The Constitution of
The State of Michigan
A Quick Reference Guide

Bootblack Budget Books
Copyright 2018 ©
ISBN-13: 978-1986640428
ISBN-10: 1986640426

Contents:

Preamble – Page 26

Article I: Declaration of Rights – Page 27

Section 1. Political power

Section 2. Equal protection; discrimination

Section 3. Assembly, consultation, instruction, petition

Section 4. Freedom of worship and religious belief; appropriations

Section 5. Freedom of speech and of press

Section 6. Bearing of arms

Section 7. Military power subordinate to civil power

Section 8. Quartering of soldiers

Section 9. Slavery and involuntary servitude

Section 10. Attainder; ex post facto laws; impairment of contracts

Section 11. Searches and seizures

Section 12. Habeas corpus

Section 13. Conduct of suits in person or by counsel

Section 14. Jury trials.

Section 15. Double jeopardy; bailable offenses; commencement of trial if bail denied; bail hearing; effective date

Section 16. Bail; fines; punishments; detention of witnesses

Section 17. Self-incrimination; due process of law; fair treatment at investigations

Section 18. Witnesses; competency, religious beliefs

Section 19. Libels, truth as defense

Section 20. Rights of accused in criminal prosecutions

Section 21 Imprisonment for debt

Section 22. Treason; definition, evidence

Section 23. Enumeration of rights not to deny others

Section 24. Rights of crime victims; enforcement; assessment against convicted defendants

Section 25. Marriage

Section 26. Affirmative action programs.

Section 27. Human embryo and embryonic stem cell research

Article II: Elections – Page 36

Section 1. Qualifications of electors; residence

Section 2. Mental incompetence; imprisonment

Section 3. Presidential electors; residence

Section 4. Place and manner of elections

Section 5. Time of elections

Section 6. Voters on tax limit increases or bond issues

Section 7. Boards of canvassers

Section 8. Recalls

Section 9. Initiative and referendum; limitations; appropriations; petitions

Section 10. Limitations on terms of office of members of the United States House of Representatives and United States Senate from Michigan

Article III: General Government – Page 41

Section 1. Seat of government

Section 2. Separation of powers of government

Section 3. Great seal

Section 4. Militia

Section 5. Intergovernmental agreements; service by public officers and employees

Section 6. Internal improvements

Section 7. Common law and statutes, continuance

Section 8. Opinions on constitutionality by supreme court

Article IV: Legislative Branch – 43

Section 1. Legislative power

Section 2. Senators, number, term

Section 3. Representatives, number, term; contiguity of districts

Section 4. Annexation or merger with a city

Section 5. Island areas, contiguity

Section 6. Commission on legislative apportionment

Section 7. Legislators; qualifications, removal from district

Section 8. Ineligibility of government officers and employees

Section 9. Civil appointments, ineligibility of legislators

Section 10. Legislators and state officers, government contracts, conflict of interest

Section 11. Legislators privileged from civil arrest and civil process; limitation; questioning for speech in either house prohibited

Section 12. State officers compensation commission

Section 13. Legislature; time of convening, sine die adjournment, measures carried over

Section 14. Quorum; powers of less than quorum

Section 15. Legislative council

Section 16. Legislature; officers, rules of procedure, expulsion of members

Section 17. Committees; record of votes, public inspection, notice of hearings

Section 18. Journal of proceedings; record of votes, dissents

Section 19. Record of votes on elections and advice and consent

Section 20. Open meetings

Section 21. Adjournments, limitations

Section 22. Bills

Section 23. Style of laws

Section 24. Laws; object, title, amendments changing purpose

Section 25. Revision and amendment of laws; title references, publication of entire sections

Section 26. Bills; printing, possession, reading, vote on passage

Section 27. Laws, effective date

Section 28. Bills, subjects at special session

Section 29. Local or special acts

Section 30. Appropriations; local or private purposes

Section 31. General appropriation bills; priority, statement of estimated revenue

Section 32. Laws imposing taxes

Section 33. Bills passed; approval by governor or veto, reconsideration by legislature

Section 34. Bills, referendum

Section 35. Publication and distribution of laws and judicial decisions

Section 36. General revision of laws; compilation of laws

Section 37. Administrative rules, suspension by legislative committee

Section 38. Vacancies in office

Section 39. Continuity of government in emergencies

Section 40. Alcoholic beverages; age requirement; liquor control commission; excise tax; local option

Section 41. Lotteries

Section 42. Ports and port districts; incorporation, internal

Section 43. Bank and trust company laws

Section 44. Trial by jury in civil cases

Section 45. Indeterminate sentences

Section 46. Death penalty

Section 47. Chaplains in state institutions

Section 48. Disputes concerning public employees

Section 49. Hours and conditions of employment

Section 50. Atomic and new forms of energy

Section 51. Public health and general welfare

Section 52. Natural resources; conservation, pollution, impairment, destruction

Section 53. Auditor general; appointment, qualifications, term, removal, post audits

Section 54. Limitations on terms of office of state legislators

Article V: Executive Branch – Page 63

Section 1. Executive power

Section 2. Principal departments

Section 3. Single heads of departments; appointment, term

Section 4. Commissions or agencies for less than 2 years

Section 5. Examining or licensing board members, qualifications

Section 6. Advice and consent to appointments

Section 7. Vacancies in office; filling, senatorial disapproval of appointees

Section 8. Principal departments, supervision of governor; information from state officers

Section 9. Principal departments, location

Section 10. Removal or suspension of officers; grounds, report

Section 11. Provisional appointments to fill vacancies due to suspension

Section 12. Military powers

Section 13. Elections to fill vacancies in legislature

Section 14. Reprieves, commutations and pardons

Section 15. Extra sessions of legislature

Section 16. Legislature other than at seat of government

Section 17. Messages and recommendations to legislature

Section 18. Budget; general and deficiency appropriation bills

Section 19. Disapproval of items in appropriation bills

Section 20. Reductions in expenditures

Section 21. State elective executive officers; term, election

Section 22. Governor and lieutenant governor, qualifications

Section 23. State elective executive officers, compensation

Section 24. Executive residence

Section 25. Lieutenant governor; president of senate, tie vote, duties, Succession to governorship

Section 26. Succession to Governorship

Section 27. Salary of Successor

Section 28. State Transportation Commission; Establishment; Purpose; Appointment, Qualifications, and Terms of Members; Director of State Transportation Department

Section 29. Civil Rights Commission; Members, Term, Duties, Appropriation

Section 30. Section 30. Limitations on Terms of Executive Officers

Article VI: Judicial Branch – Page 74

Section 1. Judicial power in court of justice; divisions

Section 2. Justices of the supreme court; number, term, nomination, election

Section 3. Chief justice; court administrator; other assistants

Section 4. General superintending control over courts; writs; appellate jurisdiction

Section 5. Court rules; distinctions between law and equity; master in chancery

Section 6. Decisions and dissents; writing, contents

Section 7. Staff; budget; salaries of justices; fees

Section 8. Court of appeals; election of judges, divisions

Section 9. Judges of court of appeals, terms

Section 10. Jurisdiction, practice and procedure of court of appeals

Section 11. Circuit courts; judicial circuits, sessions, number of judges

Section 12. Circuit judges; nomination, election, term

Section 13. Circuit courts; jurisdiction, writs, supervisory control over inferior courts

Section 14. County clerks; duties, vacancies; prosecuting attorneys, vacancies

Section 15. Probate courts; districts, jurisdiction

Section 16. Probate judges; nomination, election, terms

Section 17. Judicial salaries and fees

Section 18. Salaries; uniformity, changes during term

Section 19. Courts of record; seal, qualifications of judges

Section 20. Removal of domicile of judge

Section 21. Ineligibility for other office

Section 22. Incumbent judges, affidavit of candidacy

Section 23. Judicial vacancies, filling; appointee, term; successor; new offices

Section 24. Incumbent judges, ballot designation

Section 25. Removal of judges from office

Section 26. Circuit court commissioners and justices of the peace, abolition; courts of limited jurisdiction

Section 27. Power of appointment to public office

Section 28. Administrative action, review

Section 29. Conservators of the peace

Section 30. Judicial tenure commission; selection; terms; duties; power of supreme court

Article VII: Local Government – Page 84

Section 2. Counties; corporate character, powers and immunities

Section 2. County charters

Section 3. Reduction of size of county

Section 4. County officers; terms, combination

Section 5. Offices at county seat

Section 6. Sheriffs; security, responsibility for acts, ineligibility for other office

Section 7. Boards of supervisors; members

Section 8. Legislative, administrative, and other powers and duties of boards

Section 9. Compensation of county officers

Section 10. Removal of county seat

Section 11. Indebtedness, limitation

Section 12. Navigable streams, permission to bridge or dam

Section 13. Consolidation of counties, approval by electors

Section 14. Organization and consolidation of townships

Section 15. County intervention in public utility service and rate proceedings

Section 16. Highways, bridges, culverts, airports; road tax limitation

Section 17. Townships; corporate character, powers and Immunities

Section 18. Township officers; term, powers and duties

Section 19. Township public utility franchises

Section 20. Townships, dissolution; villages as cities

Section 21. Cities and villages; incorporation, taxes, Indebtedness

Section 22. Charters, resolutions, ordinances; enumeration of powers

Section 23. Parks, boulevards, cemeteries, hospitals

Section 24. Public service facilities

Section 25. Public utilities; acquisition, franchises, sale

Section 26. Cities and villages, loan of credit

Section 27. Metropolitan governments and authorities

Section 28. Governmental functions and powers; joint administration, costs and credits, transfers

Section 29. Highways, streets, alleys, public places; control, use by public utilities

Section 30. Franchises and licenses, duration

Section 31. Vacation or alteration of roads, streets, alleys, public places

Section 32. Budgets, public hearing

Section 33. Removal of elected officers

Section 34. Construction of constitution and law concerning counties, townships, cities, villages

Article VIII: Education – Page 94

Section 1. Encouragement of education

Section 2. Free public elementary and secondary schools; discrimination

Section 3. State board of education; duties

Section 4. Higher education institutions; appropriations, accounting, public sessions of boards

Section 5. University of Michigan, Michigan State University, Wayne State University; controlling boards

Section 6. Other institutions of higher education, controlling boards

Section 7. Community and junior colleges; state board, members, terms, vacancies

Section 8. Services for disabled persons

Section 9. Public libraries, fines

Article IX: Finance And Taxation – Page 99

Section 1. Taxes for state expenses

Section 2. Power of taxation, relinquishment

Section 3. Property taxation; uniformity; assessments; limitations; classes; approval of legislature

Section 4. Exemption of religious or educational nonprofit organizations

Section 5. Assessment of property of public service businesses

Section 6. Real and tangible personal property; limitation on general ad valorem taxes; adoption and alteration of separate tax limitations; exceptions to limitations; property tax on school district extending into 2 or more counties

Section 7. Income tax

Section 8. Sales and use taxes

Section 9. Use of specific taxes on fuels for transportation purposes; authorization of indebtedness and issuance of obligations

Section 10. Sales tax; distribution to local governments

Section 11. State school aid fund; source; distribution; guarantee to local school district

Section 12. Evidence of state indebtedness

Section 13. Public bodies, borrowing power

Section 14. State borrowing; short term

Section 15. Long term borrowing by state

Section 16. State loans to school districts

Section 17. Payments from state treasury

Section 18. State credit

Section 19. Subscription to or interest in stock by state prohibited; exceptions

Section 20. Deposit of state money in certain financial institutions; requirements

Section 21. Accounting for public moneys

Section 22. Examination and adjustment of claims against state

Section 23. Financial records; statement of revenues and expenditures

Section 24. Public pension plans and retirement systems, obligation

Section 25. Voter approval of increased local taxes; prohibitions; emergency conditions; repayment of bonded indebtedness guaranteed; implementation of section

Section 26. Limitation on taxes; revenue limit; refunding or transferring excess revenues; exceptions to revenue limitation; adjustment of state revenue and spending limits

Section 27. Exceeding revenue limit; conditions

Section 28. Limitation on expenses of state government

Section 29. State financing of activities or services required of local government by state law

Section 30. Reduction of state spending paid to units of local government

Section 31. Levying tax or increasing rate of existing tax; maximum tax rate on new base; increase in assessed valuation of property; exceptions to limitations

Section 32. Suit to enforce sections 25 to 31

Section 33. Definitions applicable to sections 25 to 32

Section 34. Implementation of sections 25 to 33

Section 35. Michigan natural resources trust fund

Section 35a. Michigan state parks endowment fund

Section 36. Tax on tobacco products; dedication of proceeds

Section 37. Michigan veterans' trust fund

Section 38. Michigan veterans' trust fund board of trustees; establishment

Section 39. Michigan veterans' trust fund board of trustees; administration of trust fund

Section 40. Michigan conservation and recreation legacy fund

Section 41. Michigan game and fish protection trust fund

Section 42. Michigan non-game fish and wildlife trust fund

Article X: Property – Page 126

Section 1. Disabilities of coverture abolished; separate property of wife; dower

Section 2. Eminent domain; compensation

Section 3. Homestead and personalty, exemption from process

Section 4. Escheats

Section 5. State lands

Section 6. Resident aliens, property rights

Article XI: Public Officers And Employment – Page 129

Section 1. Oath of public officers

Section 2. Terms of office of state and county officers

Section 3. Extra compensation

Section 4. Custodian of public moneys; eligibility to office, accounting

Section 5. Classified state civil service; scope; exempted positions; appointment and terms of members of state civil service commission; state personnel director; duties of commission; collective bargaining for state police troopers and sergeants; appointments, promotions, demotions, or removals; increases or reductions in compensation; creating or abolishing positions; recommending compensation for unclassified service; appropriation; reports of expenditures; annual audit; payment for personal services; violation; injunctive or mandamus proceedings

Section 6. Merit systems for local governments

Section 7. Impeachment of civil officers.

Section 8. Convictions for certain felonies; eligibility for elective office or certain positions of public employment

Article XII: Amendment And Revision – Page 135

Section 1. Amendment by legislative proposal and vote of electors

Section 2. Amendment by petition and vote of electors

Section 3. General revision of constitution; submission of question, convention delegates and meeting

Section 4. Severability

Schedule And Temporary Provisions – Page 139

Section 1. Recommendations by attorney general for changes in laws

Section 2. Existing public and private rights, continuance

Section 3. Officers, continuance in office

Section 4. Officers elected in spring of 1963, term

Section 5. State elective executive officers and senators, 2 and 4 year terms

Section 6. Supreme court, reduction to 7 justices

Section 7. Judges of probate, eligibility for re-election

Section 8. Judicial officers, staggered terms

Section 9. State board of education; first election, terms

Section 10. Boards controlling higher education institutions and state board of public community and junior colleges, terms

Section 11. Michigan State University trustees and Wayne State University governors, terms

Section 12. Initial allocation of departments by law or executive order

Section 13. State contracts, continuance

Section 14. Mackinac Bridge Authority; refunding of bonds, transfer of functions to highway department

Section 15. Submission of constitution; time, notice

Section 16. Voters, ballots, effective date

Section 17. Vote Record

Preamble

We, the people of the State of Michigan, grateful to Almighty God for the blessings of freedom, and earnestly desiring to secure these blessings undiminished to ourselves and our posterity, do ordain and establish this constitution.

ARTICLE I: DECLARATION OF RIGHTS

Section 1. Political Power

All political power is inherent in the people. Government is instituted for their equal benefit, security and protection.

Section 2. Equal Protection; Discrimination

No person shall be denied the equal protection of the laws; nor shall any person be denied the enjoyment of his civil or political rights or be discriminated against in the exercise thereof because of religion, race, color or national origin. The legislature shall implement this section by appropriate legislation.

Section 3. Assembly, Consultation, Instruction, Petition

The people have the right peaceably to assemble, to consult for the common good, to instruct their representatives and to petition the government for redress of grievances.

Section 4. Freedom of Worship and Religious Belief; Appropriations

Every person shall be at liberty to worship God according to the dictates of his own conscience. No person shall be compelled to attend, or, against his consent, to contribute to the erection or support of any place of religious worship, or to pay tithes, taxes or other rates for the support of any minister of the gospel or teacher of religion. No money shall be appropriated or drawn from the treasury for the benefit of any religious sect or society, theological or religious seminary; nor shall property belonging to the state be appropriated for any such purpose. The civil and political rights, privileges and capacities of no person shall be diminished or enlarged on account of his religious belief.

Section 5. Freedom Of Speech And Of Press

Every person may freely speak, write, express and publish his views on all subjects, being responsible for the abuse of such right; and no law shall be enacted to restrain or abridge the liberty of speech or of the press.

Section 6. Bearing of Arms

Every person has a right to keep and bear arms for the defense of himself and the state.

Section 7. Military Power Subordinate to Civil Power

The military shall in all cases and at all times be in strict subordination to the civil power.

Section 8. Quartering of Soldiers

No soldier shall, in time of peace, be quartered in any house without the consent of the owner or occupant, nor in time of war, except in a manner prescribed by law.

Section 9. Slavery and Involuntary Servitude

Neither slavery, nor involuntary servitude unless for the punishment of crime, shall ever be tolerated in this state.

Section 10. Attainder; Ex Post Facto Laws; Impairment of Contracts

No bill of attainder, ex post facto law or law impairing the obligation of contract shall be enacted.

Section 11. Searches and Seizures

The person, houses, papers and possessions of every person shall be secure from unreasonable searches and seizures. No warrant to search any place or to seize any person or things shall issue without describing them, nor without probable cause, supported by oath or affirmation. The provisions of this section shall not be construed to bar from evidence in any criminal proceeding any narcotic drug, firearm, bomb, explosive or any other dangerous weapon, seized by a peace officer outside the curtilage of any dwelling house in this state.

Section 12. Habeas Corpus

The privilege of the writ of habeas corpus shall not be suspended unless in case of rebellion or invasion the public safety may require it.

Section 13. Conduct of Suits in Person or by Counsel

A suitor in any court of this state has the right to prosecute or defend his suit, either in his own proper person or by an attorney.

Section 14. Jury Trials

The right of trial by jury shall remain, but shall be waived in all civil cases unless demanded by one of the parties in the manner prescribed by law. In all civil cases tried by 12 jurors a verdict shall be received when 10 jurors agree.

Section 15. Double Jeopardy; Bailable Offenses; Commencement of Trial If Bail Denied; Bail Hearing; Effective Date

No person shall be subject for the same offense to be twice put in jeopardy. All persons shall, before conviction, be bailable by sufficient sureties, except that bail may be denied for the following persons when the proof is evident or the presumption great:

(a) A person who, within the 15 years immediately preceding a motion for bail pending the disposition of an indictment for a violent felony or of an arraignment on a warrant charging a violent felony, has been convicted of 2 or more violent felonies under the laws of this state or under substantially similar laws of the United States or another state, or a combination thereof, only if the prior felony convictions arose out of at least 2 separate incidents, events, or transactions.

(b) A person who is indicted for, or arraigned on a warrant charging, murder or treason.

(c) A person who is indicted for, or arraigned on a warrant charging, criminal sexual conduct in the first degree, armed robbery, or kidnapping with intent to extort money or other valuable thing thereby, unless the court finds by clear and convincing evidence that the defendant is not likely to flee or present a danger to any other person. (d) A person who is indicted for, or arraigned on a warrant charging, a violent felony which is alleged to have been committed while the person was on bail, pending the disposition of a prior violent felony charge or while the person was on probation or parole as a result of a prior conviction for a violent felony. If a person is denied admission to bail under this section, the trial of the person shall be commenced not more than 90 days after the date on which admission to bail is denied. If the trial is not commenced within 90 days after the date on which admission to bail is denied and the delay is not attributable to the defense, the court shall immediately schedule a bail hearing and shall set the amount of bail for the person. As used in this section, "violent felony" means a felony, an element of which involves a violent act or threat of a violent act against any other person. This section, as amended, shall not take effect until May 1, 1979.

Section 16. Bail; Fines; Punishments; Detention of Witnesses

Excessive bail shall not be required; excessive fines shall not be imposed; cruel or unusual punishment shall not be inflicted; nor shall witnesses be unreasonably detained.

Section 17. Self-Incrimination; Due Process of Law; Fair Treatment at Investigations

No person shall be compelled in any criminal case to be a witness against himself, nor be deprived of life, liberty or property, without due process of law. The right of all individuals, firms, corporations and voluntary associations to fair and just treatment in the course of legislative and executive investigations and hearings shall not be infringed.

Section 18. Witnesses; Competency, Religious Beliefs

No person shall be rendered incompetent to be a witness on account of his opinions on matters of religious belief.

Section 19. Libels, Truth as Defense

In all prosecutions for libels the truth may be given in evidence to the jury; and, if it appears to the jury that the matter charged as libelous is true and was published with good motives and for justifiable ends, the accused shall be acquitted.

Section 20. Rights of Accused in Criminal Prosecutions

In every criminal prosecution, the accused shall have the right to a speedy and public trial by an impartial jury, which may consist of less than 12 jurors in prosecutions for misdemeanors punishable by imprisonment for not more than 1 year; to be informed of the nature of the accusation; to be confronted with the witnesses against him or her; to have compulsory process for obtaining witnesses in his or her favor; to have the assistance of counsel for his or her defense; to have an appeal as a matter of right, except as provided by law an appeal by an accused who pleads guilty or nolo contendere shall be by leave of the court; and as provided by law, when the trial court so orders, to have such reasonable assistance as may be necessary to perfect and prosecute an appeal

Section 21. Imprisonment for Debt

No person shall be imprisoned for debt arising out of or founded on contract, express or implied, except in cases of fraud or breach of trust.

Section 22. Treason; Definition, Evidence

Treason against the state shall consist only in levying war against it or in adhering to its enemies, giving them aid and comfort. No person shall be convicted of treason unless upon the testimony of two witnesses to the same overt act or on confession in open court.

Section 23. Enumeration of Rights not to Deny Others

The enumeration in this constitution of certain rights shall not be construed to deny or disparage others retained by the people.

Section 24. Rights of Crime Victims; Enforcement; Assessment Against Convicted Defendants

(1) Crime victims, as defined by law, shall have the following rights, as provided by law: The right to be treated with fairness and respect for their dignity and privacy throughout the criminal justice process. The right to timely disposition of the case following arrest of the accused. The right to be reasonably protected from the accused throughout the criminal justice process. The right to notification of court proceedings. The right to attend trial and all other court proceedings the accused has the right to attend. The right to confer with the prosecution. The right to make a statement to the court at sentencing. The right to restitution. The right to information about the conviction, sentence, imprisonment, and release of the accused.

(2) The legislature may provide by law for the enforcement of this section.

(3) The legislature may provide for an assessment against convicted defendants to pay for crime victims' rights.

Section 25. Marriage

To secure and preserve the benefits of marriage for our society and for future generations of children, the union of one man and one woman in marriage shall be the only agreement recognized as a marriage or similar union for any purpose.

Section 26. Affirmative Action Programs

(1) The University of Michigan, Michigan State University, Wayne State University, and any other public college or university, community college, or school district shall not discriminate against, or grant preferential treatment to, any individual or group on the basis of race, sex, color, ethnicity, or national origin in the operation of public employment, public education, or public contracting.
(2) The state shall not discriminate against, or grant preferential treatment to, any individual or group on the basis of race, sex, color, ethnicity, or national origin in the operation of public employment, public education, or public contracting.

(3) For the purposes of this section "state" includes, but is not necessarily limited to, the state itself, any city, county, any public college, university, or community college, school district, or other political subdivision or governmental instrumentality of or within the State of Michigan not included in sub-section 1.

(4) This section does not prohibit action that must be taken to establish or maintain eligibility for any federal program, if ineligibility would result in a loss of federal funds to the state.

(5) Nothing in this section shall be interpreted as prohibiting bona fide qualifications based on sex that are reasonably necessary to the normal operation of public employment, public education, or public contracting.

(6) The remedies available for violations of this section shall be the same, regardless of the injured party's race, sex, color, ethnicity, or national origin, as are otherwise available for violations of Michigan anti-discrimination law.

(7) This section shall be self-executing. If any part or parts of this section are found to be in conflict with the United States Constitution or federal law, the section shall be implemented to the maximum extent that the United States Constitution and federal law permit. Any provision held invalid shall be severable from the remaining portions of this section.

(8) This section applies only to action taken after the effective date of this section.

(9) This section does not invalidate any court order or consent decree that is in force as of the effective date of this section.

Section 27. Human Embryo and Embryonic Stem Cell Research

(1) Nothing in this section shall alter Michigan's current prohibition on human cloning.

(2) To ensure that Michigan citizens have access to stem cell therapies and cures, and to ensure that physicians and researchers can conduct the most promising forms of medical research in this state, and that all such research is conducted safely and ethically, any research permitted under federal law on human embryos may be conducted in Michigan, subject to the requirements of federal law and only the following additional limitations and requirements:

(a) No stem cells may be taken from a human embryo more than fourteen days after cell division begins; provided, however, that time during which an embryo is frozen does not count against this fourteen day limit.

(b) The human embryos were created for the purpose of fertility treatment and, with voluntary and informed consent, documented in writing, the person seeking fertility treatment chose to donate the embryos for research; and

(i) the embryos were in excess of the clinical need of the person seeking the fertility treatment and would otherwise be discarded unless they are used for research; or

(ii) the embryos were not suitable for implantation and would otherwise be discarded unless they are used for research.

(c) No person may, for valuable consideration, purchase or sell human embryos for stem cell research or stem cell therapies and cures.

(d) All stem cell research and all stem cell therapies and cures must be conducted and provided in accordance with state and local laws of general applicability, including but not limited to laws concerning scientific and medical practices and patient safety and privacy, to the extent that any such laws do not:

(i) prevent, restrict, obstruct, or discourage any stem cell research or stem cell therapies and cures that are permitted by the provisions of this section; or

(ii) create disincentives for any person to engage in or otherwise associate with such research or therapies or cures.

(3) Any provision of this section held unconstitutional shall be severable from the remaining portions of this section.

ARTICLE II: ELECTIONS

Section 1. Qualifications of Electors; Residence

Every citizen of the United States who has attained the age of 21 years, who has resided in this state six months, and who meets the requirements of local residence provided by law, shall be an elector and qualified to vote in any election except as otherwise provided in this constitution. The legislature shall define residence for voting purposes.

Section 2. Mental Incompetence; Imprisonment

The legislature may by law exclude persons from voting because of mental incompetence or commitment to a jail or penal institution.

Section 3. Presidential Electors; Residence

For purposes of voting in the election for president and vice-president of the United States only, the legislature may by law establish lesser residence requirements for citizens who have resided in this state for less than six months and may waive residence requirements for former citizens of this state who have removed herefrom. The legislature shall not permit voting by any person who meets the voting residence requirements of the state to which he has removed.

Section 4. Place and Manner of Elections

The legislature shall enact laws to regulate the time, place and manner of all nominations and elections, except as otherwise provided in this constitution or in the constitution and laws of the United States. The legislature shall enact laws to preserve the purity of elections, to preserve the secrecy of the ballot, to guard against abuses of the elective franchise, and to provide for a system of voter registration and absentee voting. No law shall be enacted which permits a candidate in any partisan primary or partisan election to have a ballot designation except when required for identification of candidates for the same office who have the same or similar surnames.

Section 5. Time of Elections

Except for special elections to fill vacancies, or as otherwise provided in this constitution, all elections for national, state, county and township offices shall be held on the first Tuesday after the first Monday in November in each even-numbered year or on such other date as members of the congress of the United States are regularly elected.

Section 6. Voters on Tax Limit Increases or Bond Issues

Whenever any question is required to be submitted by a political subdivision to the electors for the increase of the ad valorem tax rate limitation imposed by Section 6 of Article IX for a period of more than five years, or for the issue of bonds, only electors in, and who have property assessed for any ad valorem taxes in, any part of the district or territory to be affected by the result of such election or electors who are the lawful husbands or wives of such persons shall be entitled to vote thereon. All electors in the district or territory affected may vote on all other questions.

Section 7. Boards of Canvassers

A board of state canvassers of four members shall be established by law. No candidate for an office to be canvassed nor any inspector of elections shall be eligible to serve as a member of a board of canvassers. A majority of any board of canvassers shall not be composed of members of the same political party.

Section 8. Recalls

Laws shall be enacted to provide for the recall of all elective officers except judges of courts of record upon petition of electors equal in number to 25 percent of the number of persons voting in the last preceding election for the office of governor in the electoral district of the officer sought to be recalled. The sufficiency of any statement of reasons or grounds procedurally required shall be a political rather than a judicial question.

Section 9. Initiative And Referendum; Limitations; Appropriations; Petitions

The people reserve to themselves the power to propose laws and to enact and reject laws, called the initiative, and the power to approve or reject laws enacted by the legislature, called the referendum. The power of initiative extends only to laws which the legislature may enact under this constitution. The power of referendum does not extend to acts making appropriations for state institutions or to meet deficiencies in state funds and must be invoked in the manner prescribed by law within 90 days following the final adjournment of the legislative session at which the law was enacted. To invoke the initiative or referendum, petitions signed by a number of registered electors, not less than eight percent for initiative and five percent for referendum of the total vote cast for all candidates for governor at the last preceding general election at which a governor was elected shall be required.

Referendum, Approval

No law as to which the power of referendum properly has been invoked shall be effective thereafter unless approved by a majority of the electors voting thereon at the next general election.

Initiative; Duty of Legislature, Referendum

Any law proposed by initiative petition shall be either enacted or rejected by the legislature without change or amendment within 40 session days from the time such petition is received by the legislature. If any law proposed by such petition shall be enacted by the legislature it shall be subject to referendum, as hereinafter provided.

Legislative Rejection of Initiated Measure; Different Measure; Submission to People

If the law so proposed is not enacted by the legislature within the 40 days, the state officer authorized by law shall submit such proposed law to the people for approval or rejection at the next general election. The legislature may reject any measure so proposed by initiative petition and propose a different measure upon the same subject by a yea and nay vote upon separate roll calls, and in such event both measures shall be submitted by such state officer to the electors for approval or rejection at the next general election.

Initiative or Referendum Law; Effective Date, Veto, Amendment and Repeal

Any law submitted to the people by either initiative or referendum petition and approved by a majority of the votes cast thereon at any election shall take effect 10 days after the date of the official declaration of the vote. No law initiated or adopted by the people shall be subject to the veto power of the governor, and no law adopted by the people at the polls under the initiative provisions of this section shall be amended or repealed, except by a vote of the electors unless otherwise provided in the initiative measure or by three-fourths of the members elected to and serving in each house of the legislature. Laws approved by the people under the referendum provision of this section may be amended by the legislature at any subsequent session thereof. If two or more measures approved by the electors at the same election conflict, that receiving the highest affirmative vote shall prevail.

Legislative Implementation

The legislature shall implement the provisions of this section.

Section 10. Limitations on Terms of Office of Members of the United States House of Representatives and United States Senate from Michigan

No person shall be elected to office as representative in the United States House of Representatives more than three times during any twelve year period. No person shall be elected to office as senator in the United States Senate more than two times during any twenty-four year period. Any person appointed or elected to fill a vacancy in the United States House of Representatives or the United States Senate for a period greater than one half of a term of such office, shall be considered to have been elected to serve one time in that office for purposes of this section. This limitation on the number of times a person shall be elected to office shall apply to terms of office beginning on or after January 1, 1993. The people of Michigan hereby state their support for the aforementioned term limits for members of the United States House of Representatives and United States Senate and instruct their public officials to use their best efforts to attain such a limit nationwide.

The people of Michigan declare that the provisions of this section shall be deemed severable from the remainder of this amendment and that their intention is that federal officials elected from Michigan will continue voluntarily to observe the wishes of the people as stated in this section, in the event any provision of this section is held invalid. This section shall be self-executing. Legislation may be enacted to facilitate operation of this section, but no law shall limit or restrict the application of this section. If any part of this section is held to be invalid or unconstitutional, the remaining parts of this section shall not be affected but will remain in full force and effect.

ARTICLE III: GENERAL GOVERNMENT

Section 1. Seat of Government

The seat of government shall be at Lansing.

Section 2. Separation of Powers of Government

The powers of government are divided into three branches: legislative, executive and judicial. No person exercising powers of one branch shall exercise powers properly belonging to another branch except as expressly provided in this constitution.

Section 3. Great Seal

There shall be a great seal of the State of Michigan and its use shall be provided by law.

Section 4. Militia

The militia shall be organized, equipped and disciplined as provided by law.

Section 5. Intergovernmental Agreements; Service by Public Officers and Employees

Subject to provisions of general law, this state or any political subdivision thereof, any governmental authority or any combination thereof may enter into agreements for the performance, financing or execution of their respective functions, with any one or more of the other states, the United States, the Dominion of Canada, or any political subdivision thereof unless otherwise provided in this constitution. Any other provision of this constitution notwithstanding, an officer or employee of the state or of any such unit of government or subdivision or agency thereof may serve on or with any governmental body established for the purposes set forth in this section and shall not be required to relinquish his office or employment by reason of such service. The legislature may impose such restrictions, limitations or conditions on such service as it may deem appropriate.

Section 6. Internal Improvements

The state shall not be a party to, nor be financially interested in, any work of internal improvement, nor engage in carrying on any such work, except for public internal improvements provided by law.

Section 7. Common Law and Statutes, Continuance

The common law and the statute laws now in force, not repugnant to this constitution, shall remain in force until they expire by their own limitations, or are changed, amended or repealed.

Section 8. Opinions on Constitutionality by Supreme Court

Either house of the legislature or the governor may request the opinion of the supreme court on important questions of law upon solemn occasions as to the constitutionality of legislation after it has been enacted into law but before its effective date.

ARTICLE IV: LEGISLATIVE BRANCH

Section 1. Legislative Power

The legislative power of the State of Michigan is vested in a senate and a house of representatives.

Section 2. Senators, Number, Term

The senate shall consist of 38 members to be elected from single member districts at the same election as the governor for four-year terms concurrent with the term of office of the governor. Senatorial districts, apportionment factors. In districting the state for the purpose of electing senators after the official publication of the total population count of each federal decennial census, each county shall be assigned apportionment factors equal to the sum of its percentage of the state's population as shown by the last regular federal decennial census computed to the nearest one-one hundredth of one percent multiplied by four and its percentage of the state's land area computed to the nearest one-one hundredth of one percent. Apportionment rules. In arranging the state into senatorial districts, the apportionment commission shall be governed by the following rules:

(1) Counties with 13 or more apportionment factors shall be entitled as a class to senators in the proportion that the total apportionment factors of such counties bear to the total apportionment factors of the state computed to the nearest whole number. After each such county has been allocated one senator, the remaining senators to which this class of counties is entitled shall be distributed among such counties by the method of equal proportions applied to the apportionment factors.

(2) Counties having less than 13 apportionment factors shall be entitled as a class to senators in the proportion that the total apportionment factors of such counties bear to the total apportionment factors of the state computed to the nearest whole number. Such counties shall thereafter be arranged into senatorial districts that are compact, convenient, and contiguous by land, as rectangular in shape as possible, and having as nearly as possible 13 apportionment factors, but in no event less than 10 or more than 16. Insofar as possible, existing senatorial districts at the time of reapportionment shall not be altered unless there is a failure to comply with the above standards.

(3) Counties entitled to two or more senators shall be divided into single member districts. The population of such districts shall be as nearly equal as possible but shall not be less than 75 percent nor more than 125 percent of a number determined by dividing the population of the county by the number of senators to which it is entitled. Each such district shall follow incorporated city or township boundary lines to the extent possible and shall be compact, contiguous, and as nearly uniform in shape as possible.

Section 3. Representatives, Number, Term; Contiguity of Districts

The house of representatives shall consist of 110 members elected for two-year terms from single member districts apportioned on a basis of population as provided in this article. The districts shall consist of compact and convenient territory contiguous by land.

Representative Areas, Single and Multiple County

Each county which has a population of not less than seven-tenths of one percent of the population of the state shall constitute a separate representative area. Each county having less than seven-tenths of one percent of the population of the state shall be combined with another county or counties to form a representative area of not less than seven-tenths of one percent of the population of the state. Any county which is isolated under the initial allocation as provided in this section shall be joined with that contiguous representative area having the smallest percentage of the state's population. Each such representative area shall be entitled initially to one representative.

Apportionment of Representatives to Areas

After the assignment of one representative to each of the representative areas, the remaining house seats shall be apportioned among the representative areas on the basis of population by the method of equal proportions.

Districting of Single County Area Entitled to 2 or More Representatives

Any county comprising a representative area entitled to two or more representatives shall be divided into single member representative districts as follows:

(1) The population of such districts shall be as nearly equal as possible but shall not be less than 75 percent nor more than 125 percent of a number determined by dividing the population of the representative area by the number of representatives to which it is entitled.

(2) Such single member districts shall follow city and township boundaries where applicable and shall be composed of compact and contiguous territory as nearly square in shape as possible.

Districting of Multiple County Representative Areas

Any representative area consisting of more than one county, entitled to more than one representative, shall be divided into single member districts as equal as possible in population, adhering to county lines.

Section 4. Annexation or Merger with a City

In counties having more than one representative or senatorial district, the territory in the same county annexed to or merged with a city between apportionments shall become a part of a contiguous representative or senatorial district in the city with which it is combined, if provided by ordinance of the city. The district or districts with which the territory shall be combined shall be determined by such ordinance certified to the secretary of state. No such change in the boundaries of a representative or senatorial district shall have the effect of removing a legislator from office during his term.

Section 5. Island Areas, Contiguity

Island areas are considered to be contiguous by land to the county of which they are a part.

Section 6. Commission on Legislative Apportionment

A commission on legislative apportionment is hereby established consisting of eight electors, four of whom shall be selected by the state organizations of each of the two political parties whose candidates for governor received the highest vote at the last general election at which a governor was elected preceding each apportionment. If a candidate for governor of a third political party has received at such election more than 25 percent of such gubernatorial vote, the commission shall consist of 12 members, four of whom shall be selected by the state organization of the third political party. One resident of each of the following four regions shall be selected by each political party organization:

(1) The Upper Peninsula;

(2) the northern part of the lower peninsula, north of a line drawn along the northern boundaries of the counties of Bay, Midland, Isabella, Mecosta, Newaygo and Oceana;

(3) southwestern Michigan, those counties south of region (2) and west of a line drawn along the western boundaries of the counties of Bay, Saginaw, Shiawassee, Ingham, Jackson and Hillsdale;

(4) southeastern Michigan, the remaining counties of the state.

Eligibility to Membership

No officers or employees of the federal, state or local governments, excepting notaries public and members of the armed forces reserve, shall be eligible for membership on the commission. Members of the commission shall not be eligible for election to the legislature until two years after the apportionment in which they participated becomes effective.

Appointment, Term, Vacancies

The commission shall be appointed immediately after the adoption of this constitution and whenever apportionment or districting of the legislature is required by the provisions of this constitution. Members of the commission shall hold office until each apportionment or districting plan becomes effective. Vacancies shall be filled in the same manner as for original appointment.

Officers, Rules of Procedure, Compensation, Appropriation

The secretary of state shall be secretary of the commission without vote, and in that capacity shall furnish, under the direction of the commission, all necessary technical services. The commission shall elect its own chairman, shall make its own rules of procedure, and shall receive compensation provided by law. The legislature shall appropriate funds to enable the commission to carry out its activities.

Call To Convene; Apportionment; Public Hearings

Within 30 days after the adoption of this constitution, and after the official total population count of each federal decennial census of the state and its political subdivisions is available, the secretary of state shall issue a call convening the commission not less than 30 nor more than 45 days thereafter. The commission shall complete its work within 180 days after all necessary census information is available. The commission shall proceed to district and apportion the senate and house of representatives according to the provisions of this constitution. All final decisions shall require the concurrence of a majority of the members of the commission. The commission shall hold public hearings as may be provided by law.

Apportionment Plan, Publication; Record of Proceedings

Each final apportionment and districting plan shall be published as provided by law within 30 days from the date of its adoption and shall become law 60 days after publication. The secretary of state shall keep a public record of all the proceedings of the commission and shall be responsible for the publication and distribution of each plan.

Disagreement of Commission; Submission of Plans to Supreme Court

If a majority of the commission cannot agree on a plan, each member of the commission, individually or jointly with other members, may submit a proposed plan to the supreme court. The supreme court shall determine which plan complies most accurately with the constitutional requirements and shall direct that it be adopted by the commission and published as provided in this section.

Jurisdiction of Supreme Court on Elector's Application

Upon the application of any elector filed not later than 60 days after final publication of the plan, the supreme court, in the exercise of original jurisdiction, shall direct the secretary of state or the commission to perform their duties, may review any final plan adopted by the commission, and shall remand such plan to the commission for further action if it fails to comply with the requirements of this constitution.

Section 7. Legislators; Qualifications, Removal From District

Each senator and representative must be a citizen of the United States, at least 21 years of age, and an elector of the district he represents. The removal of his domicile from the district shall be deemed a vacation of the office. No person who has been convicted of subversion or who has within the preceding 20 years been convicted of a felony involving a breach of public trust shall be eligible for either house of the legislature.

Section 8. Ineligibility of Government Officers and Employees

No person holding any office, employment or position under the United States or this state or a political subdivision thereof, except notaries public and members of the armed forces reserve, may be a member of either house of the legislature.

Section 9. Civil Appointments, Ineligibility of Legislators

No person elected to the legislature shall receive any civil appointment within this state from the governor, except notaries public, from the legislature, or from any other state authority, during the term for which he is elected.

Section 10. Legislators and State Officers, Government Contracts, Conflict of Interest

No member of the legislature nor any state officer shall be interested directly or indirectly in any contract with the state or any political subdivision thereof which shall cause a substantial conflict of interest. The legislature shall further implement this provision by appropriate legislation.

Section 11. Legislators Privileged From Civil Arrest and Civil Process; Limitation; Questioning for Speech in Either House Prohibited

Except as provided by law, senators and representatives shall be privileged from civil arrest and civil process during sessions of the legislature and for five days next before the commencement and after the termination thereof. They shall not be questioned in any other place for any speech in either house.

Section 12. State Officers Compensation Commission

The state officers compensation commission is created which subject to this section shall determine the salaries and expense allowances of the members of the legislature, the governor, the lieutenant governor, the attorney general, the secretary of state, and the justices of the supreme court. The commission shall consist of 7 members appointed by the governor whose qualifications may be determined by law. Subject to the legislature's ability to amend the commission's determinations as provided in this section, the commission shall determine the salaries and expense allowances of the members of the legislature, the governor, the lieutenant governor, the attorney general, the secretary of state, and the justices of the supreme court which determinations shall be the salaries and expense allowances only if the legislature by concurrent resolution adopted by a majority of the members elected to and serving in each house of the legislature approve them. The senate and house of representatives shall alternate on which house of the legislature shall originate the concurrent resolution, with the senate originating the first concurrent resolution. The concurrent resolution may amend the salary and expense determinations of the state officers compensation commission to reduce the salary and expense determinations by the same proportion for members of the legislature, the governor, the lieutenant governor, the attorney general, the secretary of state, and the justices of the supreme court. The legislature shall not amend the salary and expense determinations to reduce them to below the salary and expense level that members of the legislature, the governor, the lieutenant governor, the attorney general, the secretary of state, and the justices of the supreme court receive on the date the salary and expense determinations are made. If the salary and expense determinations are approved or amended as provided in this section, the salary and expense determinations shall become effective for the legislative session immediately following the next general election. The commission shall meet each 2 years for no more than 15 session days. The legislature shall implement this section by law.

Section 13. Legislature; Time of Convening, Sine Die Adjournment, Measures Carried Over

The legislature shall meet at the seat of government on the second Wednesday in January of each year at twelve o'clock noon. Each regular session shall adjourn without day, on a day determined by concurrent resolution, at twelve o'clock noon. Any business, bill or joint resolution pending at the final adjournment of a regular session held in an odd numbered year shall carry over with the same status to the next regular session.

Section 14. Quorum; powers of less than quorum

A majority of the members elected to and serving in each house shall constitute a quorum to do business. A smaller number in each house may adjourn from day to day, and may compel the attendance of absent members in the manner and with penalties as each house may prescribe.

Section 15. Legislative Council

There shall be a bi-partisan legislative council consisting of legislators appointed in the manner prescribed by law. The legislature shall appropriate funds for the council's operations and provide for its staff which shall maintain bill drafting, research and other services for the members of the legislature. The council shall periodically examine and recommend to the legislature revision of the various laws of the state.

Section 16. Legislature; Officers, Rules of Procedure, Expulsion of Members

Each house, except as otherwise provided in this constitution, shall choose its own officers and determine the rules of its proceedings, but shall not adopt any rule that will prevent a majority of the members elected thereto and serving therein from discharging a committee from the further consideration of any measure. Each house shall be the sole judge of the qualifications, elections and returns of its members, and may, with the concurrence of two-thirds of all the members elected thereto and serving therein, expel a member. The reasons for such expulsion shall be entered in the journal, with the votes and names of the members voting upon the question. No member shall be expelled a second time for the same cause.

Section 17. Committees; Record of Votes, Public Inspection, Notice of Hearings

Each house of the legislature may establish the committees necessary for the efficient conduct of its business and the legislature may create joint committees. On all actions on bills and resolutions in each committee, names and votes of members shall be recorded. Such vote shall be available for public inspection. Notice of all committee hearings and a clear statement of all subjects to be considered at each hearing shall be published in the journal in advance of the hearing.

Section 18. Journal of Proceedings; Record of Votes, Dissents

Each house shall keep a journal of its proceedings, and publish the same unless the public security otherwise requires. The record of the vote and name of the members of either house voting on any question shall be entered in the journal at the request of one-fifth of the members present. Any member of either house may dissent from and protest against any act, proceeding or resolution which he deems injurious to any person or the public, and have the reason for his dissent entered in the journal.

Section 19. Record of Votes on Elections and Advice and Consent

All elections in either house or in joint convention and all votes on appointments submitted to the senate for advice and consent shall be published by vote and name in the journal.

Section 20. Open Meetings

The doors of each house shall be open unless the public security otherwise requires.

Section 21. Adjournments, Limitations

Neither house shall, without the consent of the other, adjourn for more than two intervening calendar days, nor to any place other than where the legislature may then be in session.

Section 22. Bills

All legislation shall be by bill and may originate in either house.

Section 23. Style of Laws

The style of the laws shall be: The People of the State of Michigan enact.

Section 24. Laws; Object, Title, Amendments Changing Purpose

No law shall embrace more than one object, which shall be expressed in its title. No bill shall be altered or amended on its passage through either house so as to change its original purpose as determined by its total content and not alone by its title.

Section 25. Revision and Amendment of Laws; Title References, Publication of Entire Sections

No law shall be revised, altered or amended by reference to its title only. The section or sections of the act altered or amended shall be re-enacted and published at length.

Section 26. Bills; Printing, Possession, Reading, Vote on Passage

No bill shall be passed or become a law at any regular session of the legislature until it has been printed or reproduced and in the possession of each house for at least five days. Every bill shall be read three times in each house before the final passage thereof. No bill shall become a law without the concurrence of a majority of the members elected to and serving in each house. On the final passage of bills, the votes and names of the members voting thereon shall be entered in the journal.

Section 27. Laws, Effective Date

No act shall take effect until the expiration of 90 days from the end of the session at which it was passed, but the legislature may give immediate effect to acts by a two-thirds vote of the members elected to and serving in each house.

Section 28. Bills, Subjects at Special Session

When the legislature is convened on extraordinary occasions in special session no bill shall be passed on any subjects other than those expressly stated in the governor's proclamation or submitted by special message.

Section 29. Local or Special Acts

The legislature shall pass no local or special act in any case where a general act can be made applicable, and whether a general act can be made applicable shall be a judicial question. No local or special act shall take effect until approved by two-thirds of the members elected to and serving in each house and by a majority of the electors voting thereon in the district affected. Any act repealing local or special acts shall require only a majority of the members elected to and serving in each house and shall not require submission to the electors of such district.

Section 30. Appropriations; Local or Private Purposes

The assent of two-thirds of the members elected to and serving in each house of the legislature shall be required for the appropriation of public money or property for local or private purposes.

Section 31. General Appropriation Bills; Priority, Statement of Estimated Revenue

The general appropriation bills for the succeeding fiscal period covering items set forth in the budget shall be passed or rejected in either house of the legislature before that house passes any appropriation bill for items not in the budget except bills supplementing appropriations for the current fiscal year's operation. Any bill requiring an appropriation to carry out its purpose shall be considered an appropriation bill. One of the general appropriation bills as passed by the legislature shall contain an itemized statement of estimated revenue by major source in each operating fund for the ensuing fiscal period, the total of which shall not be less than the total of all appropriations made from each fund in the general appropriation bills as passed.

Section 32. Laws Imposing Taxes

Every law which imposes, continues or revives a tax shall distinctly state the tax.

Section 33. Bills Passed; Approval by Governor or Veto, Reconsideration by Legislature

Every bill passed by the legislature shall be presented to the governor before it becomes law, and the governor shall have 14 days measured in hours and minutes from the time of presentation in which to consider it. If he approves, he shall within that time sign and file it with the secretary of state and it shall become law. If he does not approve, and the legislature has within that time finally adjourned the session at which the bill was passed, it shall not become law. If he disapproves, and the legislature continues the session at which the bill was passed, he shall return it within such 14-day period with his objections, to the house in which it originated. That house shall enter such objections in full in its journal and reconsider the bill. If two-thirds of the members elected to and serving in that house pass the bill notwithstanding the objections of the governor, it shall be sent with the objections to the other house for reconsideration. The bill shall become law if passed by two-thirds of the members elected to and serving in that house. The vote of each house shall be entered in the journal with the votes and names of the members voting thereon. If any bill is not returned by the governor within such 14-day period, the legislature continuing in session, it shall become law as if he had signed it.

Section 34. Bills, Referendum

Any bill passed by the legislature and approved by the governor, except a bill appropriating money, may provide that it will not become law unless approved by a majority of the electors voting thereon.

Section 35. Publication and Distribution of Laws and Judicial Decisions

All laws enacted at any session of the legislature shall be published in book form within 60 days after final adjournment of the session, and shall be distributed in the manner provided by law. The prompt publication of judicial decisions shall be provided by law. All laws and judicial decisions shall be free for publication by any person.

Section 36. General Revision of Laws; Compilation of Laws

No general revision of the laws shall be made. The legislature may provide for a compilation of the laws in force, arranged without alteration, under appropriate heads and titles.

Section 37. Administrative Rules, Suspension by Legislative Committee

The legislature may by concurrent resolution empower a joint committee of the legislature, acting between sessions, to suspend any rule or regulation promulgated by an administrative agency subsequent to the adjournment of the last preceding regular legislative session. Such suspension shall continue no longer than the end of the next regular legislative session.

Section 38. Vacancies in Office

The legislature may provide by law the cases in which any office shall be vacant and the manner of filling vacancies where no provision is made in this constitution.

Section 39. Continuity of Government in Emergencies

In order to insure continuity of state and local governmental operations in periods of emergency only, resulting from disasters occurring in this state caused by enemy attack on the United States, the legislature may provide by law for prompt and temporary succession to the powers and duties of public offices, of whatever nature and whether filled by election or appointment, the incumbents of which may become unavailable for carrying on the powers and duties of such offices; and enact other laws necessary and proper for insuring the continuity of governmental operations. Notwithstanding the power conferred by this section, elections shall always be called as soon as possible to fill any vacancies in elective offices temporarily occupied by operation of any legislation enacted pursuant to the provisions of this section.

Section 40. Alcoholic Beverages; Age Requirement; Liquor Control Commission; Excise Tax; Local Option

A person shall not sell or give any alcoholic beverage to any person who has not reached the age of 21 years. A person who has not reached the age of 21 years shall not possess any alcoholic beverage for the purpose of personal consumption. An alcoholic beverage is any beverage containing one-half of one percent or more alcohol by volume. Except as prohibited by this section, (t)he legislature may by law establish a liquor control commission which, subject to statutory limitations, shall exercise complete control of the alcoholic beverage traffic within this state, including the retail sales thereof. The legislature may provide for an excise tax on such sales. Neither the legislature nor the commission may authorize the manufacture or sale of alcoholic beverages in any county in which a majority of the electors voting thereon shall prohibit the same.

Section 41. Lotteries

The legislature may authorize lotteries and permit the sale of lottery tickets in the manner provided by law. No law enacted after January 1, 2004, that authorizes any form of gambling shall be effective, nor after January 1, 2004, shall any new state lottery games utilizing table games or player operated mechanical or electronic devices be established, without the approval of a majority of electors voting in a statewide general election and a majority of electors voting in the township or city where gambling will take place. This section shall not apply to gambling in up to three casinos in the City of Detroit or to Indian tribal gaming.

Section 42. Ports and Port Districts; Incorporation, Internal

The legislature may provide for the incorporation of ports and port districts, and confer power and authority upon them to engage in work of internal improvements in connection therewith.

Section 43. Bank and Trust Company Laws

No general law providing for the incorporation of trust companies or corporations for banking purposes, or regulating the business thereof, shall be enacted, amended or repealed except by a vote of two-thirds of the members elected to and serving in each house.

Section 44. Trial By Jury in Civil Cases

The legislature may authorize a trial by a jury of less than 12 jurors in civil cases.

Section 45. Indeterminate Sentences

The legislature may provide for indeterminate sentences as punishment for crime and for the detention and release of persons imprisoned or detained under such sentences.

Section 46. Death Penalty

No law shall be enacted providing for the penalty of death.

Section 47. Chaplains in State Institutions

The legislature may authorize the employment of chaplains in state institutions of detention or confinement.

Section 48. Disputes Concerning Public Employees

The legislature may enact laws providing for the resolution of disputes concerning public employees, except those in the state classified civil service.

Section 49. Hours and Conditions of Employment

The legislature may enact laws relative to the hours and conditions of employment.

Section 50. Atomic and New Forms of Energy

The legislature may provide safety measures and regulate the use of atomic energy and forms of energy developed in the future, having in view the general welfare of the people of this state.

Section 51. Public Health And General Welfare

The public health and general welfare of the people of the state are hereby declared to be matters of primary public concern. The legislature shall pass suitable laws for the protection and promotion of the public health.

Section 52. Natural Resources; Conservation, Pollution, Impairment, Destruction

The conservation and development of the natural resources of the state are hereby declared to be of paramount public concern in the interest of the health, safety and general welfare of the people. The legislature shall provide for the protection of the air, water and other natural resources of the state from pollution, impairment and destruction.

Section 53. Auditor General; Appointment, Qualifications, Term, Removal, Post Audits

The legislature by a majority vote of the members elected to and serving in each house, shall appoint an auditor general, who shall be a certified public accountant licensed to practice in this state, to serve for a term of eight years. He shall be ineligible for appointment or election to any other public office in this state from which compensation is derived while serving as auditor general and for two years following the termination of his service. He may be removed for cause at any time by a two-thirds vote of the members elected to and serving in each house. The auditor general shall conduct post audits of financial transactions and accounts of the state and of all branches, departments, offices, boards, commissions, agencies, authorities and institutions of the state established by this constitution or by law, and performance post audits thereof.

Independent Investigations; Reports

The auditor general upon direction by the legislature may employ independent accounting firms or legal counsel and may make investigations pertinent to the conduct of audits. He shall report annually to the legislature and to the governor and at such other times as he deems necessary or as required by the legislature. He shall be assigned no duties other than those specified in this section.

Governing Boards of Institutions of Higher Education

Nothing in this section shall be construed in any way to infringe the responsibility and constitutional authority of the governing boards of the institutions of higher education to be solely responsible for the control and direction of all expenditures from the institutions' funds.

Staff Members, Civil Service

The auditor general, his deputy and one other member of his staff shall be exempt from classified civil service. All other members of his staff shall have classified civil service status.

Section 54. Limitations on Terms Of Office of State Legislators

No person shall be elected to the office of state representative more than three times. No person shall be elected to the office of state senate more than two times. Any person appointed or elected to fill a vacancy in the house of representatives or the state senate for a period greater than one half of a term of such office, shall be considered to have been elected to serve one time in that office for purposes of this section. This limitation on the number of times a person shall be elected to office shall apply to terms of office beginning on or after January 1, 1993.

This section shall be self-executing. Legislation may be enacted to facilitate operation of this section, but no law shall limit or restrict the application of this section. If any part of this section is held to be invalid or unconstitutional, the remaining parts of this section shall not be affected but will remain in full force and effect.

ARTICLE V: EXECUTIVE BRANCH

Section 1. Executive Power

The executive power is vested in the governor.

Section 2. Principal Departments

All executive and administrative offices, agencies and instrumentalities of the executive branch of state government and their respective functions, powers and duties, except for the office of governor and lieutenant governor and the governing bodies of institutions of higher education provided for in this constitution, shall be allocated by law among and within not more than 20 principal departments. They shall be grouped as far as practicable according to major purposes. Organization of executive branch; assignment of functions; submission to legislature. Subsequent to the initial allocation, the governor may make changes in the organization of the executive branch or in the assignment of functions among its units which he considers necessary for efficient administration. Where these changes require the force of law, they shall be set forth in executive orders and submitted to the legislature. Thereafter the legislature shall have 60 calendar days of a regular session, or a full regular session if of shorter duration, to disapprove each executive order. Unless disapproved in both houses by a resolution concurred in by a majority of the members elected to and serving in each house, each order shall become effective at a date thereafter to be designated by the governor.

Section 3. Single Heads of Departments; Appointment, Term

The head of each principal department shall be a single executive unless otherwise provided in this constitution or by law. The single executives heading principal departments shall include a secretary of state, a state treasurer and an attorney general. When a single executive is the head of a principal department, unless elected or appointed as otherwise provided in this constitution, he shall be appointed by the governor by and with the advice and consent of the senate and he shall serve at the pleasure of the governor.

Boards Heading Departments; Appointment, Term, Removal

When a board or commission is at the head of a principal department, unless elected or appointed as otherwise provided in this constitution, the members thereof shall be appointed by the governor by and with the advice and consent of the senate. The term of office and procedure for removal of such members shall be as prescribed in this constitution or by law.

Boards and Commissions, Maximum Term

Terms of office of any board or commission created or enlarged after the effective date of this constitution shall not exceed four years except as otherwise authorized in this constitution. The terms of office of existing boards and commissions which are longer than four years shall not be further extended except as provided in this constitution.

Section 4. Commissions or Agencies for less than 2 Years

Temporary commissions or agencies for special purposes with a life of no more than two years may be established by law and need not be allocated within a principal department.

Section 5. Examining or Licensing Board Members, Qualifications

A majority of the members of an appointed examining or licensing board of a profession shall be members of that profession.

Section 6. Advice and Consent to Appointments

Appointment by and with the advice and consent of the senate when used in this constitution or laws in effect or hereafter enacted means appointment subject to disapproval by a majority vote of the members elected to and serving in the senate if such action is taken within 60 session days after the date of such appointment. Any appointment not disapproved within such period shall stand confirmed.

Section 7. Vacancies in Office; Filling, Senatorial Disapproval of Appointees

Vacancies in any office, appointment to which requires advice and consent of the senate, shall be filled by the governor by and with the advice and consent of the senate. A person whose appointment has been disapproved by the senate shall not be eligible for an interim appointment to the same office.

Section 8. Principal Departments, Supervision of Governor; Information from State Officers

Each principal department shall be under the supervision of the governor unless otherwise provided by this constitution. The governor shall take care that the laws be faithfully executed. He shall transact all necessary business with the officers of government and may require information in writing from all executive and administrative state officers, elective and appointive, upon any subject relating to the duties of their respective offices.

Court Enforcement of Constitutional or Legislative Mandate

The governor may initiate court proceedings in the name of the state to enforce compliance with any constitutional or legislative mandate, or to restrain violations of any constitutional or legislative power, duty or right by any officer, department or agency of the state or any of its political subdivisions. This authority shall not be construed to authorize court proceedings against the legislature.

Section 9. Principal Departments, Location

Single executives heading principal departments and the chief executive officers of principal departments headed by boards or commissions shall keep their offices at the seat of government except as otherwise provided by law, superintend them in person and perform duties prescribed by law.

Section 10. Removal or Suspension of Officers; Grounds, Report

The governor shall have power and it shall be his duty to inquire into the condition and administration of any public office and the acts of any public officer, elective or appointive. He may remove or suspend from office for gross neglect of duty or for corrupt conduct in office, or for any other misfeasance or malfeasance therein, any elective or appointive state officer, except legislative or judicial, and shall report the reasons for such removal or suspension to the legislature.

Section 11. Provisional Appointments to Fill Vacancies Due to Suspension

The governor may make a provisional appointment to fill a vacancy occasioned by the suspension of an appointed or elected officer, other than a legislative or judicial officer, until he is reinstated or until the vacancy is filled in the manner prescribed by law or this constitution.

Section 12. Military Powers

The governor shall be commander-in-chief of the armed forces and may call them out to execute the laws, suppress insurrection and repel invasion.

Section 13. Elections to Fill Vacancies in Legislature

The governor shall issue writs of election to fill vacancies in the senate or house of representatives. Any such election shall be held in a manner prescribed by law.

Section 14. Reprieves, Commutations and Pardons

The governor shall have power to grant reprieves, commutations and pardons after convictions for all offenses, except cases of impeachment, upon such conditions and limitations as he may direct, subject to procedures and regulations prescribed by law. He shall inform the legislature annually of each reprieve, commutation and pardon granted, stating reasons therefor.

Section 15. Extra Sessions of Legislature

The governor may convene the legislature on extraordinary occasions.

Section 16. Legislature other than at Seat of Government

The governor may convene the legislature at some other place when the seat of government becomes dangerous from any cause.

Section 17. Messages and Recommendations to Legislature

The governor shall communicate by message to the legislature at the beginning of each session and may at other times present to the legislature information as to the affairs of the state and recommend measures he considers necessary or desirable.

Section 18. Budget; General and Deficiency Appropriation Bills

The governor shall submit to the legislature at a time fixed by law, a budget for the ensuing fiscal period setting forth in detail, for all operating funds, the proposed expenditures and estimated revenue of the state. Proposed expenditures from any fund shall not exceed the estimated revenue thereof. On the same date, the governor shall submit to the legislature general appropriation bills to embody the proposed expenditures and any necessary bill or bills to provide new or additional revenues to meet proposed expenditures. The amount of any surplus created or deficit incurred in any fund during the last preceding fiscal period shall be entered as an item in the budget and in one of the appropriation bills. The governor may submit amendments to appropriation bills to be offered in either house during consideration of the bill by that house, and shall submit bills to meet deficiencies in current appropriations.

Section 19. Disapproval of Items in Appropriation Bills

The governor may disapprove any distinct item or items appropriating moneys in any appropriation bill. The part or parts approved shall become law, and the item or items disapproved shall be void unless re-passed according to the method prescribed for the passage of other bills over the executive veto.

Section 20. Reductions in Expenditures

No appropriation shall be a mandate to spend. The governor, with the approval of the appropriating committees of the house and senate, shall reduce expenditures authorized by appropriations whenever it appears that actual revenues for a fiscal period will fall below the revenue estimates on which appropriations for that period were based. Reductions in expenditures shall be made in accordance with procedures prescribed by law. The governor may not reduce expenditures of the legislative and judicial branches or from funds constitutionally dedicated for specific purposes.

Section 21. State Elective Executive Officers; Term, Election

The governor, lieutenant governor, secretary of state and attorney general shall be elected for four-year terms at the general election in each alternate even-numbered year.

Lieutenant Governor, Secretary of State and Attorney General, Nomination.

The lieutenant governor, secretary of state and attorney general shall be nominated by party conventions in a manner prescribed by law. In the general election one vote shall be cast jointly for the candidates for governor and lieutenant governor nominated by the same party.

Secretary of State and Attorney General, Vacancies in Office

Vacancies in the office of the secretary of state and attorney general shall be filled by appointment by the governor.

Section 22. Governor and Lieutenant Governor, Qualifications

To be eligible for the office of governor or lieutenant governor a person must have attained the age of 30 years, and have been a registered elector in this state for four years next preceding his election.

Section 23. State Elective Executive Officers, Compensation

The governor, lieutenant governor, secretary of state and attorney general shall each receive the compensation provided by law in full payment for all services performed and expenses incurred during his term of office. Such compensation shall not be changed during the term of office except as otherwise provided in this constitution.

Section 24. Executive Residence

An executive residence suitably furnished shall be provided at the seat of government for the use of the governor. He shall receive an allowance for its maintenance as provided by law.

Section 25. Lieutenant Governor; President of Senate, Tie Vote, Duties

The lieutenant governor shall be president of the senate, but shall have no vote, unless they be equally divided. He may perform duties requested of him by the governor, but no power vested in the governor shall be delegated.

Section 26. Succession to Governorship

In case of the conviction of the governor on impeachment, his removal from office, his resignation or his death, the lieutenant governor, the elected secretary of state, the elected attorney general and such other persons designated by law shall in that order be governor for the remainder of the governor's term.

Death of Governor-Elect

In case of the death of the governor-elect, the lieutenant governor-elect, the secretary of state-elect, the attorney general-elect and such other persons designated by law shall become governor in that order at the commencement of the governor-elect's term.

Duration of Successor's Term as Governor

If the governor or the person in line of succession to serve as governor is absent from the state, or suffering under an inability, the powers and duties of the office of the governor shall devolve in order of precedence until the absence or inability giving rise to the devolution of powers ceases.

Determination of Inability

The inability of the governor or person acting as governor shall be determined by a majority of the supreme court on joint request of the president pro tempore of the senate and the speaker of the house of representatives. Such determination shall be final and conclusive. The supreme court shall upon its own initiative determine if and when the inability ceases.

Section 27. Salary of Successor

The legislature shall provide that the salary of any state officer while acting as governor shall be equal to that of the governor.

Section 28. State Transportation Commission; Establishment; Purpose; Appointment, Qualifications, and Terms of Members; Director of State Transportation Department

There is hereby established a state transportation commission, which shall establish policy for the state transportation department transportation programs and facilities, and such other public works of the state, as provided by law. The state transportation commission shall consist of six members, not more than three of whom shall be members of the same political party. They shall be appointed by the governor by and with the advice and consent of the senate for three-year terms, no three of which shall expire in the same year, as provided by law. The director of the state transportation department shall be appointed as provided by law and shall be the principal executive officer of the state transportation department and shall be responsible for executing the policy of the state transportation commission.

Section 29. Civil Rights Commission; Members, Term, Duties, Appropriation

There is hereby established a civil rights commission which shall consist of eight persons, not more than four of whom shall be members of the same political party, who shall be appointed by the governor, by and with the advice and consent of the senate, for four-year terms not more than two of which shall expire in the same year. It shall be the duty of the commission in a manner which may be prescribed by law to investigate alleged discrimination against any person because of religion, race, color or national origin in the enjoyment of the civil rights guaranteed by law and by this constitution, and to secure the equal protection of such civil rights without such discrimination. The legislature shall provide an annual appropriation for the effective operation of the commission.

Rules And Regulations; Hearings, Orders

The commission shall have power, in accordance with the provisions of this constitution and of general laws governing administrative agencies, to promulgate rules and regulations for its own procedures, to hold hearings, administer oaths, through court authorization to require the attendance of witnesses and the submission of records, to take testimony, and to issue appropriate orders. The commission shall have other powers provided by law to carry out its purposes. Nothing contained in this section shall be construed to diminish the right of any party to direct and immediate legal or equitable remedies in the courts of this state.

Appeals

Appeals from final orders of the commission, including cease and desist orders and refusals to issue complaints, shall be tried de novo before the circuit court having jurisdiction provided by law.

Section 30. Limitations on Terms of Executive Officers

No person shall be elected more than two times to each office of the executive branch of government: governor, lieutenant governor, secretary of state or attorney general. Any person appointed or elected to fill a vacancy in the office of governor, lieutenant governor, secretary of state or attorney general for a period greater than one half of a term of such office, shall be considered to have been elected to serve one time in that office for purposes of this section. This limitation on the number of times a person shall be elected to office shall apply to terms of office beginning on or after January 1, 1993. This section shall be self-executing. Legislation may be enacted to facilitate operation of this section, but no law shall limit or restrict the application of this section. If any part of this section is held to be invalid or unconstitutional, the remaining parts of this section shall not be affected but will remain in full force and effect.

ARTICLE VI: JUDICIAL BRANCH

Section 1. Judicial Power in Court of Justice; Divisions

The judicial power of the state is vested exclusively in one court of justice which shall be divided into one supreme court, one court of appeals, one trial court of general jurisdiction known as the circuit court, one probate court, and courts of limited jurisdiction that the legislature may establish by a two-thirds vote of the members elected to and serving in each house.

Section 2. Justices Of The Supreme Court; Number, Term, Nomination, Election

The supreme court shall consist of seven justices elected at non-partisan elections as provided by law. The term of office shall be eight years and not more than two terms of office shall expire at the same time. Nominations for justices of the supreme court shall be in the manner prescribed by law. Any incumbent justice whose term is to expire may become a candidate for re-election by filing an affidavit of candidacy, in the form and manner prescribed by law, not less than 180 days prior to the expiration of his term.

Section 3. Chief Justice; Court Administrator; Other Assistants

One justice of the supreme court shall be selected by the court as its chief justice as provided by rules of the court. He shall perform duties required by the court. The supreme court shall appoint an administrator of the courts and other assistants of the supreme court as may be necessary to aid in the administration of the courts of this state. The administrator shall perform administrative duties assigned by the court.

Section 4. General Superintending Control Over Courts; Writs; Appellate Jurisdiction

The supreme court shall have general superintending control over all courts; power to issue, hear and determine prerogative and remedial writs; and appellate jurisdiction as provided by rules of the supreme court. The supreme court shall not have the power to remove a judge.

Section 5. Court Rules; Distinctions Between Law and Equity; Master in Chancery

The supreme court shall by general rules establish, modify, amend and simplify the practice and procedure in all courts of this state. The distinctions between law and equity proceedings shall, as far as practicable, be abolished. The office of master in chancery is prohibited.

Section 6. Decisions and Dissents; Writing, Contents

Decisions of the supreme court, including all decisions on prerogative writs, shall be in writing and shall contain a concise statement of the facts and reasons for each decision and reasons for each denial of leave to appeal. When a judge dissents in whole or in part he shall give in writing the reasons for his dissent.

Section 7. Staff; Budget; Salaries of Justices; Fees

The supreme court may appoint, may remove, and shall have general supervision of its staff. It shall have control of the preparation of its budget recommendations and the expenditure of moneys appropriated for any purpose pertaining to the operation of the court or the performance of activities of its staff except that the salaries of the justices shall be established by law. All fees and perquisites collected by the court staff shall be turned over to the state treasury and credited to the general fund.

Section 8. Court of Appeals; Election of Judges, Divisions

The court of appeals shall consist initially of nine judges who shall be nominated and elected at non-partisan elections from districts drawn on county lines and as nearly as possible of equal population, as provided by law. The supreme court may prescribe by rule that the court of appeals sit in divisions and for the terms of court and the times and places thereof. Each such division shall consist of not fewer than three judges. The number of judges comprising the court of appeals may be increased, and the districts from which they are elected may be changed by law.

Section 9. Judges of Court of Appeals, Terms

Judges of the court of appeals shall hold office for a term of six years and until their successors are elected and qualified. The terms of office for the judges in each district shall be arranged by law to provide that not all terms will expire at the same time.

Section 10. Jurisdiction, Practice and Procedure of Court of Appeals

The jurisdiction of the court of appeals shall be provided by law and the practice and procedure therein shall be prescribed by rules of the supreme court.

Section 11. Circuit Courts; Judicial Circuits, Sessions, Number of Judges

The state shall be divided into judicial circuits along county lines in each of which there shall be elected one or more circuit judges as provided by law. Sessions of the circuit court shall be held at least four times in each year in every county organized for judicial purposes. Each circuit judge shall hold court in the county or counties within the circuit in which he is elected, and in other circuits as may be provided by rules of the supreme court. The number of judges may be changed and circuits may be created, altered and discontinued by law and the number of judges shall be changed and circuits shall be created, altered and discontinued on recommendation of the supreme court to reflect changes in judicial activity. No change in the number of judges or alteration or discontinuance of a circuit shall have the effect of removing a judge from office during his term.

Section 12. Circuit Judges; Nomination, Election, Term

Circuit judges shall be nominated and elected at non-partisan elections in the circuit in which they reside, and shall hold office for a term of six years and until their successors are elected and qualified. In circuits having more than one circuit judge their terms of office shall be arranged by law to provide that not all terms will expire at the same time.

Section 13. Circuit Courts; Jurisdiction, Writs, Supervisory Control Over Inferior Courts

The circuit court shall have original jurisdiction in all matters not prohibited by law; appellate jurisdiction from all inferior courts and tribunals except as otherwise provided by law; power to issue, hear and determine prerogative and remedial writs; supervisory and general control over inferior courts and tribunals within their respective jurisdictions in accordance with rules of the supreme court; and jurisdiction of other cases and matters as provided by rules of the supreme court.

Section 14. County Clerks; Duties, Vacancies; Prosecuting Attorneys, Vacancies

The clerk of each county organized for judicial purposes or other officer performing the duties of such office as provided in a county charter shall be clerk of the circuit court for such county. The judges of the circuit court may fill a vacancy in an elective office of county clerk or prosecuting attorney within their respective jurisdictions.

Section 15. Probate Courts; Districts, Jurisdiction

In each county organized for judicial purposes there shall be a probate court. The legislature may create or alter probate court districts of more than one county if approved in each affected county by a majority of the electors voting on the question. The legislature may provide for the combination of the office of probate judge with any judicial office of limited jurisdiction within a county with supplemental salary as provided by law. The jurisdiction, powers and duties of the probate court and of the judges thereof shall be provided by law. They shall have original jurisdiction in all cases of juvenile delinquents and dependents, except as otherwise provided by law.

Section 16. Probate judges; Nomination, Election, Terms

One or more judges of probate as provided by law shall be nominated and elected at non-partisan elections in the counties or the probate districts in which they reside and shall hold office for terms of six years and until their successors are elected and qualified. In counties or districts with more than one judge the terms of office shall be arranged by law to provide that not all terms will expire at the same time.

Section 17. Judicial Salaries and Fees

No judge or justice of any court of this state shall be paid from the fees of his office nor shall the amount of his salary be measured by fees, other moneys received or the amount of judicial activity of his office.

Section 18. Salaries; Uniformity, Changes During Term

Salaries of justices of the supreme court, of the judges of the court of appeals, of the circuit judges within a circuit, and of the probate judges within a county or district, shall be uniform, and may be increased but shall not be decreased during a term of office except and only to the extent of a general salary reduction in all other branches of government.

Circuit Judges, Additional Salary from County

Each of the judges of the circuit court shall receive an annual salary as provided by law. In addition to the salary received from the state, each circuit judge may receive from any county in which he regularly holds court an additional salary as determined from time to time by the board of supervisors of the county. In any county where an additional salary is granted, it shall be paid at the same rate to all circuit judges regularly holding court therein.

Section 19. Courts of Record; Seal, Qualifications of Judges

(1) The supreme court, the court of appeals, the circuit court, the probate court and other courts designated as such by the legislature shall be courts of record and each shall have a common seal. Justices and judges of courts of record must be persons who are licensed to practice law in this state.

(2) To be qualified to serve as a judge of a trial court, a judge of the court of appeals, or a justice of the supreme court, a person shall have been admitted to the practice of law for at least 5 years. This subsection shall not apply to any judge or justice appointed or elected to judicial office prior to the date on which this subsection becomes part of the constitution.

(3) No person shall be elected or appointed to a judicial office after reaching the age of 70 years.

Section 20. Removal of Domicile of Judge

Whenever a justice or judge removes his domicile beyond the limits of the territory from which he was elected or appointed, he shall have vacated his office.

Section 21. Ineligibility for other Office

Any justice or judge of a court of record shall be ineligible to be nominated for or elected to an elective office other than a judicial office during the period of his service and for one year thereafter.

Section 22. Incumbent Judges, Affidavit of Candidacy

Any judge of the court of appeals, circuit court or probate court may become a candidate in the primary election for the office of which he is the incumbent by filing an affidavit of candidacy in the form and manner prescribed by law.

Section 23. Judicial Vacancies, Filling; Appointee, Term; Successor; New Offices

A vacancy shall occur in the office of judge of any court of record or in the district court by death, removal, resignation or vacating of the office, and such vacancy shall be filled by appointment by the governor. The person appointed by the governor shall hold office until 12 noon of the first day of January next succeeding the first general election held after the vacancy occurs, at which election a successor shall be elected for the remainder of the unexpired term. Whenever a new office of judge in a court of record, or the district court, is created by law, it shall be filled by election as provided by law. The supreme court may authorize persons who have been elected and served as judges to perform judicial duties for limited periods or specific assignments.

Section 24. Incumbent Judges, Ballot Designation

There shall be printed upon the ballot under the name of each incumbent justice or judge who is a candidate for nomination or election to the same office the designation of that office.

Section 25. Removal of Judges from Office

For reasonable cause, which is not sufficient ground for impeachment, the governor shall remove any judge on a concurrent resolution of two-thirds of the members elected to and serving in each house of the legislature. The cause for removal shall be stated at length in the resolution.

Section 26. Circuit Court Commissioners and Justices of The Peace, Abolition; Courts of Limited Jurisdiction

The offices of circuit court commissioner and justice of the peace are abolished at the expiration of five years from the date this constitution becomes effective or may within this period be abolished by law. Their jurisdiction, compensation and powers within this period shall be as provided by law. Within this five-year period, the legislature shall establish a court or courts of limited jurisdiction with powers and jurisdiction defined by law. The location of such court or courts, and the qualifications, tenure, method of election and salary of the judges of such court or courts, and by what governmental units the judges shall be paid, shall be provided by law, subject to the limitations contained in this article.

Present Statutory Courts

Statutory courts in existence at the time this constitution becomes effective shall retain their powers and jurisdiction, except as provided by law, until they are abolished by law.

Section 28. Administrative Action, Review

All final decisions, findings, rulings and orders of any administrative officer or agency existing under the constitution or by law, which are judicial or quasi-judicial and affect private rights or licenses, shall be subject to direct review by the courts as provided by law. This review shall include, as a minimum, the determination whether such final decisions, findings, rulings and orders are authorized by law; and, in cases in which a hearing is required, whether the same are supported by competent, material and substantial evidence on the whole record. Findings of fact in workmen's compensation proceedings shall be conclusive in the absence of fraud unless otherwise provided by law.

Property Tax Valuation or Allocation; Review

In the absence of fraud, error of law or the adoption of wrong principles, no appeal may be taken to any court from any final agency provided for the administration of property tax laws from any decision relating to valuation or allocation.

Section 29. Conservators of the Peace

Justices of the supreme court, judges of the court of appeals, circuit judges and other judges as provided by law shall be conservators of the peace within their respective jurisdictions.

Section 30. Judicial Tenure Commission; Selection; Terms; Duties; Power of Supreme Court

(1) A judicial tenure commission is established consisting of nine persons selected for three-year terms as follows: Four members shall be judges elected by the judges of the courts in which they serve; one shall be a court of appeals judge, one a circuit judge, one a probate judge and one a judge of a court of limited jurisdiction. Three shall be members of the state bar who shall be elected by the members of the state bar of whom one shall be a judge and two shall not be judges. Two shall be appointed by the governor; the members appointed by the governor shall not be judges, retired judges or members of the state bar. Terms shall be staggered as provided by rule of the supreme court. Vacancies shall be filled by the appointing power.

(2) On recommendation of the judicial tenure commission, the supreme court may censure, suspend with or without salary, retire or remove a judge for conviction of a felony, physical or mental disability which prevents the performance of judicial duties, misconduct in office, persistent failure to perform his duties, habitual intemperance or conduct that is clearly prejudicial to the administration of justice. The supreme court shall make rules implementing this section and providing for confidentiality and privilege of proceedings.

ARTICLE VII: LOCAL GOVERNMENT

Section 1. Counties; Corporate Character, Powers and Immunities

Each organized county shall be a body corporate with powers and immunities provided by law.

Section 2. County Charters

Any county may frame, adopt, amend or repeal a county charter in a manner and with powers and limitations to be provided by general law, which shall among other things provide for the election of a charter commission. The law may permit the organization of county government in form different from that set forth in this constitution and shall limit the rate of ad valorem property taxation for county purposes, and restrict the powers of charter counties to borrow money and contract debts. Each charter county is hereby granted power to levy other taxes for county purposes subject to limitations and prohibitions set forth in this constitution or law. Subject to law, a county charter may authorize the county through its regularly constituted authority to adopt resolutions and ordinances relating to its concerns.

Election of Charter Commissions

The board of supervisors by a majority vote of its members may, and upon petition of five percent of the electors shall, place upon the ballot the question of electing a commission to frame a charter.

Approval of Electors

No county charter shall be adopted, amended or repealed until approved by a majority of electors voting on the question.

Section 3. Reduction of Size of County

No organized county shall be reduced by the organization of new counties to less than 16 townships as surveyed by the United States, unless approved in the manner prescribed by law by a majority of electors voting thereon in each county to be affected.

Section 4. County Officers; Terms, Combination

There shall be elected for four-year terms in each organized county a sheriff, a county clerk, a county treasurer, a register of deeds and a prosecuting attorney, whose duties and powers shall be provided by law. The board of supervisors in any county may combine the offices of county clerk and register of deeds in one office or separate the same at pleasure.

Section 5. Offices at County Seat

The sheriff, county clerk, county treasurer and register of deeds shall hold their principal offices at the county seat.

Section 6. Sheriffs; Security, Responsibility for Acts, Ineligibility for Other Office

The sheriff may be required by law to renew his security periodically and in default of giving such security, his office shall be vacant. The county shall never be responsible for his acts, except that the board of supervisors may protect him against claims by prisoners for unintentional injuries received while in his custody. He shall not hold any other office except in civil defense.

Section 7. Boards of Supervisors; Members

A board of supervisors shall be established in each organized county consisting of one member from each organized township and such representation from cities as provided by law.

Section 8. Legislative, Administrative, and Other Powers and Duties of Boards

Boards of supervisors shall have legislative, administrative and such other powers and duties as provided by law.

Section 9. Compensation of County Officers

Boards of supervisors shall have exclusive power to fix the compensation of county officers not otherwise provided by law.

Section 10. Removal of County Seat

A county seat once established shall not be removed until the place to which it is proposed to be moved shall be designated by two-thirds of the members of the board of supervisors and a majority of the electors voting thereon shall have approved the proposed location in the manner prescribed by law.

Section 11. Indebtedness, Limitation

No county shall incur any indebtedness which shall increase its total debt beyond 10 percent of its assessed valuation.

Section 12. Navigable Streams, Permission to Bridge or Dam

A navigable stream shall not be bridged or dammed without permission granted by the board of supervisors of the county as provided by law, which permission shall be subject to such reasonable compensation and other conditions as may seem best suited to safeguard the rights and interests of the county and political subdivisions therein.

Section 13. Consolidation of Counties, Approval by Electors

Two or more contiguous counties may combine into a single county if approved in each affected county by a majority of the electors voting on the question.

Section 14. Organization and Consolidation of Townships

The board of supervisors of each organized county may organize and consolidate townships under restrictions and limitations provided by law.

Section 15. County Intervention in Public Utility Service and Rate Proceedings

Any county, when authorized by its board of supervisors shall have the authority to enter or to intervene in any action or certificate proceeding involving the services, charges or rates of any privately owned public utility furnishing services or commodities to rate payers within the county.

Section 16. Highways, Bridges, Culverts, Airports; Road Tax Limitation

The legislature may provide for the laying out, construction, improvement and maintenance of highways, bridges, culverts and airports by the state and by the counties and townships thereof; and may authorize counties to take charge and control of any highway within their limits for such purposes. The legislature may provide the powers and duties of counties in relation to highways, bridges, culverts and airports; may provide for county road commissioners to be appointed or elected, with powers and duties provided by law. The ad valorem property tax imposed for road purposes by any county shall not exceed in any year one-half of one percent of the assessed valuation for the preceding year.

Section 17. Townships; Corporate Character, Powers and Immunities

Each organized township shall be a body corporate with powers and immunities provided by law.

Section 18. Township Officers; Term, Powers and Duties

In each organized township there shall be elected for terms of not less than two nor more than four years as prescribed by law a supervisor, a clerk, a treasurer, and not to exceed four trustees, whose legislative and administrative powers and duties shall be provided by law.

Section 19. Township Public Utility Franchises

No organized township shall grant any public utility franchise which is not subject to revocation at the will of the township, unless the proposition shall first have been approved by a majority of the electors of such township voting thereon at a regular or special election.

Section 20. Townships, Dissolution; Villages as Cities

The legislature shall provide by law for the dissolution of township government whenever all the territory of an organized township is included within the boundaries of a village or villages notwithstanding that a village may include territory within another organized township and provide by law for the classification of such village or villages as cities.

Section 21. Cities and Villages; Incorporation, Taxes, Indebtedness

The legislature shall provide by general laws for the incorporation of cities and villages. Such laws shall limit their rate of ad valorem property taxation for municipal purposes, and restrict the powers of cities and villages to borrow money and contract debts. Each city and village is granted power to levy other taxes for public purposes, subject to limitations and prohibitions provided by this constitution or by law.

Section 22. Charters, Resolutions, Ordinances; Enumeration of Powers

Under general laws the electors of each city and village shall have the power and authority to frame, adopt and amend its charter, and to amend an existing charter of the city or village heretofore granted or enacted by the legislature for the government of the city or village. Each such city and village shall have power to adopt resolutions and ordinances relating to its municipal concerns, property and government, subject to the constitution and law. No enumeration of powers granted to cities and villages in this constitution shall limit or restrict the general grant of authority conferred by this section.

Section 23. Parks, Boulevards, Cemeteries, Hospitals

Any city or village may acquire, own, establish and maintain, within or without its corporate limits, parks, boulevards, cemeteries, hospitals and all works which involve the public health or safety.

Section 24. Public Service Facilities

Subject to this constitution, any city or village may acquire, own or operate, within or without its corporate limits, public service facilities for supplying water, light, heat, power, sewage disposal and transportation to the municipality and the inhabitants thereof.

Services Outside Corporate Limits

Any city or village may sell and deliver heat, power or light without its corporate limits in an amount not exceeding 25 percent of that furnished by it within the corporate limits, except as greater amounts may be permitted by law; may sell and deliver water and provide sewage disposal services outside of its corporate limits in such amount as may be determined by the legislative body of the city or village; and may operate transportation lines outside the municipality within such limits as may be prescribed by law.

Section 25. Public Utilities; Acquisition, Franchises, Sale

No city or village shall acquire any public utility furnishing light, heat or power, or grant any public utility franchise which is not subject to revocation at the will of the city or village, unless the proposition shall first have been approved by three-fifths of the electors voting thereon. No city or village may sell any public utility unless the proposition shall first have been approved by a majority of the electors voting thereon, or a greater number if the charter shall so provide.

Section 26. Cities and Villages, Loan of Credit

Except as otherwise provided in this constitution, no city or village shall have the power to loan its credit for any private purpose or, except as provided by law, for any public purpose.

Section 27. Metropolitan Governments and Authorities

Notwithstanding any other provision of this constitution the legislature may establish in metropolitan areas additional forms of government or authorities with powers, duties and jurisdictions as the legislature shall provide. Wherever possible, such additional forms of government or authorities shall be designed to perform multipurpose functions rather than a single function.

Section 28. Governmental Functions and Powers; Joint Administration, Costs and Credits, Transfers

The legislature by general law shall authorize two or more counties, townships, cities, villages or districts, or any combination thereof among other things to: enter into contractual undertakings or agreements with one another or with the state or with any combination thereof for the joint administration of any of the functions or powers which each would have the power to perform separately; share the costs and responsibilities of functions and services with one another or with the state or with any combination thereof which each would have the power to perform separately; transfer functions or responsibilities to one another or any combination thereof upon the consent of each unit involved; cooperate with one another and with state government; lend their credit to one another or any combination thereof as provided by law in connection with any authorized publicly owned undertaking.

Officers, Eligibility

Any other provision of this constitution notwithstanding, an officer or employee of the state or any such unit of government or subdivision or agency thereof, except members of the legislature, may serve on or with any governmental body established for the purposes set forth in this section and shall not be required to relinquish his office or employment by reason of such service.

Section 29. Highways, Streets, Alleys, Public Places; Control, Use by Public Utilities

No person, partnership, association or corporation, public or private, operating a public utility shall have the right to the use of the highways, streets, alleys or other public places of any county, township, city or village for wires, poles, pipes, tracks, conduits or other utility facilities, without the consent of the duly constituted authority of the county, township, city or village; or to transact local business therein without first obtaining a franchise from the township, city or village. Except as otherwise provided in this constitution the right of all counties, townships, cities and villages to the reasonable control of their highways, streets, alleys and public places is hereby reserved to such local units of government.

Section 30. Franchises and Licenses, Duration

No franchise or license shall be granted by any township, city or village for a period longer than 30 years.

Section 31. Vacation or Alteration of Roads, Streets, Alleys, Public Places

The legislature shall not vacate or alter any road, street, alley or public place under the jurisdiction of any county, township, city or village.

Section 32. Budgets, Public Hearing

Any county, township, city, village, authority or school district empowered by the legislature or by this constitution to prepare budgets of estimated expenditures and revenues shall adopt such budgets only after a public hearing in a manner prescribed by law.

Section 33. Removal of Elected Officers

Any elected officer of a political subdivision may be removed from office in the manner and for the causes provided by law.

Section 34. Construction of Constitution and Law Concerning Counties, Townships, Cities, Villages

The provisions of this constitution and law concerning counties, townships, cities and villages shall be liberally construed in their favor. Powers granted to counties and townships by this constitution and by law shall include those fairly implied and not prohibited by this constitution.

ARTICLE VIII: EDUCATION

Section 1. Encouragement of Education

Religion, morality and knowledge being necessary to good government and the happiness of mankind, schools and the means of education shall forever be encouraged.

Section 2. Free Public Elementary and Secondary Schools; Discrimination

The legislature shall maintain and support a system of free public elementary and secondary schools as defined by law. Every school district shall provide for the education of its pupils without discrimination as to religion, creed, race, color or national origin.

Nonpublic Schools, Prohibited Aid

No public monies or property shall be appropriated or paid or any public credit utilized, by the legislature or any other political subdivision or agency of the state directly or indirectly to aid or maintain any private, denominational or other nonpublic, pre-elementary, elementary, or secondary school. No payment, credit, tax benefit, exemption or deductions, tuition voucher, subsidy, grant or loan of public monies or property shall be provided, directly or indirectly, to support the attendance of any student or the employment of any person at any such nonpublic school or at any location or institution where instruction is offered in whole or in part to such nonpublic school students. The legislature may provide for the transportation of students to and from any school.

Section 3. State Board of Education; Duties

Leadership and general supervision over all public education, including adult education and instructional programs in state institutions, except as to institutions of higher education granting baccalaureate degrees, is vested in a state board of education. It shall serve as the general planning and coordinating body for all public education, including higher education, and shall advise the legislature as to the financial requirements in connection therewith.

Superintendent of Public Instruction; Appointment, Powers, Duties

The state board of education shall appoint a superintendent of public instruction whose term of office shall be determined by the board. He shall be the chairman of the board without the right to vote, and shall be responsible for the execution of its policies. He shall be the principal executive officer of a state department of education which shall have powers and duties provided by law.

State Board of Education; Members, Nomination, Election, Term

The state board of education shall consist of eight members who shall be nominated by party conventions and elected at large for terms of eight years as prescribed by law. The governor shall fill any vacancy by appointment for the unexpired term. The governor shall be ex-officio a member of the state board of education without the right to vote.

Boards of Institutions Of Higher Education, Limitation

The power of the boards of institutions of higher education provided in this constitution to supervise their respective institutions and control and direct the expenditure of the institutions' funds shall not be limited by this section.

Section 4. Higher Education Institutions; Appropriations, Accounting, Public Sessions of Boards

The legislature shall appropriate moneys to maintain the University of Michigan, Michigan State University, Wayne State University, Eastern Michigan University, Michigan College of Science and Technology, Central Michigan University, Northern Michigan University, Western Michigan University, Ferris Institute, Grand Valley State College, by whatever names such institutions may hereafter be known, and other institutions of higher education established by law. The legislature shall be given an annual accounting of all income and expenditures by each of these educational institutions. Formal sessions of governing boards of such institutions shall be open to the public.

Section 5. University of Michigan, Michigan State University, Wayne State University; Controlling Boards

The regents of the University of Michigan and their successors in office shall constitute a body corporate known as the Regents of the University of Michigan; the trustees of Michigan State University and their successors in office shall constitute a body corporate known as the Board of Trustees of Michigan State University; the governors of Wayne State University and their successors in office shall constitute a body corporate known as the Board of Governors of Wayne State University. Each board shall have general supervision of its institution and the control and direction of all expenditures from the institution's funds. Each board shall, as often as necessary, elect a president of the institution under its supervision. He shall be the principal executive officer of the institution, be ex-officio a member of the board without the right to vote and preside at meetings of the board. The board of each institution shall consist of eight members who shall hold office for terms of eight years and who shall be elected as provided by law. The governor shall fill board vacancies by appointment. Each appointee shall hold office until a successor has been nominated and elected as provided by law.

Section 6. Other Institutions of Higher Education, Controlling Boards

Other institutions of higher education established by law having authority to grant baccalaureate degrees shall each be governed by a board of control which shall be a body corporate. The board shall have general supervision of the institution and the control and direction of all expenditures from the institution's funds. It shall, as often as necessary, elect a president of the institution under its supervision. He shall be the principal executive officer of the institution and be ex-officio a member of the board without the right to vote. The board may elect one of its members or may designate the president, to preside at board meetings. Each board of control shall consist of eight members who shall hold office for terms of eight years, not more than two of which shall expire in the same year, and who shall be appointed by the governor by and with the advice and consent of the senate. Vacancies shall be filled in like manner.

Section 7. Community and Junior Colleges; State Board, Members, Terms, Vacancies

The legislature shall provide by law for the establishment and financial support of public community and junior colleges which shall be supervised and controlled by locally elected boards. The legislature shall provide by law for a state board for public community and junior colleges which shall advise the state board of education concerning general supervision and planning for such colleges and requests for annual appropriations for their support. The board shall consist of eight members who shall hold office for terms of eight years, not more than two of which shall expire in the same year, and who shall be appointed by the state board of education. Vacancies shall be filled in like manner. The superintendent of public instruction shall be ex-officio a member of this board without the right to vote.

Section 8. Services for Disabled Persons

Institutions, programs, and services for the care, treatment, education, or rehabilitation of those inhabitants who are physically, mentally, or otherwise seriously disabled shall always be fostered and supported.

Section 9. Public Libraries, Fines

The legislature shall provide by law for the establishment and support of public libraries which shall be available to all residents of the state under regulations adopted by the governing bodies thereof. All fines assessed and collected in the several counties, townships and cities for any breach of the penal laws shall be exclusively applied to the support of such public libraries, and county law libraries as provided by law.

ARTICLE IX: FINANCE AND TAXATION

Section 1. Taxes for State Expenses

The legislature shall impose taxes sufficient with other resources to pay the expenses of state government.

Section 2. Power of Taxation, Relinquishment

The power of taxation shall never be surrendered, suspended or contracted away.

Section 3. Property Taxation; Uniformity; Assessments; Limitations; Classes; Approval of Legislature

The legislature shall provide for the uniform general ad valorem taxation of real and tangible personal property not exempt by law except for taxes levied for school operating purposes. The legislature shall provide for the determination of true cash value of such property; the proportion of true cash value at which such property shall be uniformly assessed, which shall not, after January 1, 1966, exceed 50 percent; and for a system of equalization of assessments. For taxes levied in 1995 and each year thereafter, the legislature shall provide that the taxable value of each parcel of property adjusted for additions and losses, shall not increase each year by more than the increase in the immediately preceding year in the general price level, as defined in section 33 of this article, or 5 percent, whichever is less until ownership of the parcel of property is transferred. When ownership of the parcel of property is transferred as defined by law, the parcel shall be assessed at the applicable proportion of current true cash value. The legislature may provide for alternative means of taxation of designated real and tangible personal property in lieu of general ad valorem taxation. Every tax other than the general ad valorem property tax shall be uniform upon the class or classes on which it operates. A law that increases the statutory limits in effect as of February 1, 1994 on the maximum amount of ad valorem property taxes that may be levied for school district operating purposes requires the approval of 3/4 of the members elected to and serving in the Senate and in the House of Representatives.

Section 4. Exemption of Religious or Educational Nonprofit Organizations

Property owned and occupied by non-profit religious or educational organizations and used exclusively for religious or educational purposes, as defined by law, shall be exempt from real and personal property taxes.

Section 5. Assessment of Property of Public Service Businesses

The legislature shall provide for the assessment by the state of the property of those public service businesses assessed by the state at the date this constitution becomes effective, and of other property as designated by the legislature, and for the imposition and collection of taxes thereon. Property assessed by the state shall be assessed at the same proportion of its true cash value as the legislature shall specify for property subject to general ad valorem taxation. The rate of taxation on such property shall be the average rate levied upon other commercial, industrial, and utility property in this state under the general ad valorem tax law, or, if the legislature provides, the rate of tax applicable to the property of each business enterprise assessed by the state shall be the average rate of ad valorem taxation levied upon other commercial, industrial, and utility property in all counties in which any of such property is situated.

Section 6. Real and Tangible Personal Property; Limitation on General Ad Valorem Taxes; Adoption and Alteration of Separate Tax Limitations; Exceptions to Limitations; Property Tax on School District Extending Into 2 or More Counties

Except as otherwise provided in this constitution, the total amount of general ad valorem taxes imposed upon real and tangible personal property for all purposes in any one year shall not exceed 15 mills on each dollar of the assessed valuation of property as finally equalized. Under procedures provided by law, which shall guarantee the right of initiative, separate tax limitations for any county and for the townships and for school districts therein, the aggregate of which shall not exceed 18 mills on each dollar of such valuation, may be adopted and thereafter altered by the vote of a majority of the qualified electors of such county voting thereon, in lieu of the limitation hereinbefore established. These limitations may be increased to an aggregate of not to exceed 50 mills on each dollar of valuation, for a period of not to exceed 20 years at any one time, if approved by a majority of the electors, qualified under Section 6 of Article II of this constitution, voting on the question. The foregoing limitations shall not apply to taxes imposed for the payment of principal and interest on bonds approved by the electors or other evidences of indebtedness approved by the electors or for the payment of assessments or contract obligations in anticipation of which bonds are issued approved by the electors, which taxes may be imposed without limitation as to rate or amount; or, subject to the provisions of Section 25 through 34 of this article, to taxes imposed for any other purpose by any city, village, charter county, charter township, charter authority or other authority, the tax limitations of which are provided by charter or by general law. In any school district which extends into two or more counties, property taxes at the highest rate available in the county which contains the greatest part of the area of the district may be imposed and collected for school purposes throughout the district.

Section 7. Income Tax

No income tax graduated as to rate or base shall be imposed by the state or any of its subdivisions.

Section 8. Sales and Use Taxes

Except as provided in this section, the Legislature shall not impose a sales tax on retailers at a rate of more than 4% of their gross taxable sales of tangible personal property. Beginning May 1, 1994, the sales tax shall be imposed on retailers at an additional rate of 2% of their gross taxable sales of tangible personal property not exempt by law and the use tax at an additional rate of 2%. The proceeds of the sales and use taxes imposed at the additional rate of 2% shall be deposited in the state school aid fund established in Section 11. of this article. The allocation of sales tax revenue required or authorized by sections 9 and 10 of this article does not apply to the revenue from the sales tax imposed at the additional rate of 2%. No sales tax or use tax shall be charged or collected from and after January 1, 1975 on the sale or use of prescription drugs for human use, or on the sale or use of food for human consumption except in the case of prepared food intended for immediate consumption as defined by law. This provision shall not apply to alcoholic beverages.

Section 9. Use of Specific Taxes on Fuels for Transportation Purposes; Authorization of Indebtedness and Issuance of Obligations

All specific taxes, except general sales and use taxes and regulatory fees, imposed directly or indirectly on fuels sold or used to propel motor vehicles upon highways and to propel aircraft and on registered motor vehicles and aircraft shall, after the payment of necessary collection expenses, be used exclusively for transportation purposes as set forth in this section. Not less than 90 percent of the specific taxes, except general sales and use taxes and regulatory fees, imposed directly or indirectly on fuels sold or used to propel motor vehicles upon highways and on registered motor vehicles shall, after the payment of necessary collection expenses, be used exclusively for the transportation purposes of planning, administering, constructing, reconstructing, financing, and maintaining state, county, city, and village roads, streets, and bridges designed primarily for the use of motor vehicles using tires, and reasonable appurtenances to those state, county, city, and village roads, streets, and bridges. The balance, if any, of the specific taxes, except general sales and use taxes and regulatory fees, imposed directly or indirectly on fuels sold or used to propel motor vehicles upon highways and on registered motor vehicles, after the payment of necessary collection expenses; 100 percent of the specific taxes, except general sales and use taxes and regulatory fees, imposed directly or indirectly on fuels sold or used to propel aircraft and on registered aircraft, after the payment of necessary collection expenses; and not more than 25 percent of the general sales taxes, imposed directly or indirectly on fuels sold to propel motor vehicles upon highways, on the sale of motor vehicles, and on the sale of the parts and accessories of motor vehicles, after the payment of necessary collection expenses; shall be used exclusively for the transportation purposes of comprehensive transportation purposes as defined by law. The legislature may authorize the incurrence of indebtedness and the issuance of obligations pledging the taxes allocated or authorized to be allocated by this section, which obligations shall not be construed to be evidences of state indebtedness under this constitution.

Section 10. Sales Tax; Distribution to Local Governments

Fifteen percent of all taxes imposed on retailers on taxable sales at retail of tangible personal property at a rate of not more than 4% shall be used exclusively for assistance to townships, cities and villages, on a population basis as provided by law. In determining population the legislature may exclude any portion of the total number of persons who are wards, patients or convicts in any tax supported institution.

Section 11. State School Aid Fund; Source; Distribution; Guarantee to Local School District

There shall be established a state school aid fund which shall be used exclusively for aid to school districts, higher education, and school employees' retirement systems, as provided by law. Sixty percent of all taxes imposed at a rate of 4% on retailers on taxable sales at retail of tangible personal property, 100% of the proceeds of the sales and use taxes imposed at the additional rate of 2% provided for in Section 8. of this article, and other tax revenues provided by law, shall be dedicated to this fund. Payments from this fund shall be made in full on a scheduled basis, as provided by law. Beginning in the 1995-96 state fiscal year and each state fiscal year after 1995-96, the state shall guarantee that the total state and local per pupil revenue for school operating purposes for each local school district shall not be less than the 1994-95 total state and local per pupil revenue for school operating purposes for that local school district, as adjusted for consolidations, annexations, or other boundary changes. However, this guarantee does not apply in a year in which the local school district levies a millage rate for school district operating purposes less than it levied in 1994.

Section 12. Evidence of State Indebtedness

No evidence of state indebtedness shall be issued except for debts authorized pursuant to this constitution.

Section 13. Public Bodies, Borrowing Power

Public bodies corporate shall have power to borrow money and to issue their securities evidencing debt, subject to this constitution and law.

Section 14. State Borrowing; Short Term

To meet obligations incurred pursuant to appropriations for any fiscal year, the legislature may by law authorize the state to issue its full faith and credit notes in which case it shall pledge undedicated revenues to be received within the same fiscal year for the repayment thereof. Such indebtedness in any fiscal year shall not exceed 15 percent of undedicated revenues received by the state during the preceding fiscal year and such debts shall be repaid at the time the revenues so pledged are received, but not later than the end of the same fiscal year.

Section 15. Long Term Borrowing by State

The state may borrow money for specific purposes in amounts as may be provided by acts of the legislature adopted by a vote of two-thirds of the members elected to and serving in each house, and approved by a majority of the electors voting thereon at any general election. The question submitted to the electors shall state the amount to be borrowed, the specific purpose to which the funds shall be devoted, and the method of repayment.

Section 16. State Loans to School Districts

The state, in addition to any other borrowing power, may borrow from time to time such amounts as shall be required, pledge its faith and credit and issue its notes or bonds therefor, for the purpose of making loans to school districts as provided in this section.

Amount of Loans

If the minimum amount which would otherwise be necessary for a school district to levy in any year to pay principal and interest on its qualified bonds, including any necessary allowances for estimated tax delinquencies, exceeds 13 mills on each dollar of its assessed valuation as finally equalized, or such lower millage as the legislature may prescribe, then the school district may elect to borrow all or any part of the excess from the state. In that event the state shall lend the excess amount to the school district for the payment of principal and interest. If for any reason any school district will be or is unable to pay the principal and interest on its qualified bonds when due, then the school district shall borrow and the state shall lend to it an amount sufficient to enable the school district to make the payment.

Qualified Bonds

The term "qualified bonds" means general obligation bonds of school districts issued for capital expenditures, including refunding bonds, issued prior to May 4, 1955, or issued thereafter and qualified as provided by law pursuant to Section 27 or Section 28 of Article X of the Constitution of 1908 or pursuant to this section.

Repayment of Loans, Tax Levy by School District

After a school district has received loans from the state, each year thereafter it shall levy for debt service, exclusive of levies for nonqualified bonds, not less than 13 mills or such lower millage as the legislature may prescribe, until the amount loaned has been repaid, and any tax collections therefrom in any year over and above the minimum requirements for principal and interest on qualified bonds shall be used toward the repayment of state loans. In any year when such levy would produce an amount in excess of the requirements and the amount due to the state, the levy may be reduced by the amount of the excess.

Bonds, State Loans, Repayment

Subject to the foregoing provisions, the legislature shall have the power to prescribe and to limit the procedure, terms and conditions for the qualification of bonds, for obtaining and making state loans, and for the repayment of loans.

Power to Tax Unlimited

The power to tax for the payment of principal and interest on bonds hereafter issued which are the general obligations of any school district, including refunding bonds, and for repayment of any state loans made to school districts, shall be without limitation as to rate or amount.

Rights and Obligations to Remain Unimpaired

All rights acquired under Sections 27 and 28 of Article X of the Constitution of 1908, by holders of bonds heretofore issued, and all obligations assumed by the state or any school district under these sections, shall remain unimpaired.

Section 17. Payments from State Treasury

No money shall be paid out of the state treasury except in pursuance of appropriations made by law.

Section 18. State Credit

The credit of the state shall not be granted to, nor in aid of any person, association or corporation, public or private, except as authorized in this constitution. Investment of public funds. This section shall not be construed to prohibit the investment of public funds until needed for current requirements or the investment of funds accumulated to provide retirement or pension benefits for public officials and employees, as provided by law.

Section 19. Subscription to or Interest in Stock by State Prohibited; Exceptions

The state shall not subscribe to, nor be interested in the stock of any company, association or corporation, except as follows:

(a) Funds accumulated to provide retirement or pension benefits for public officials and employees may be invested as provided by law.

(b) Endowment funds created for charitable or educational purposes may be invested as provided by law governing the investment of funds held in trust by trustees.

(c) Funds held as permanent funds or endowment funds other than those described in subdivision (b) may be invested as provided by law. Except as otherwise provided in this section, other state funds or money may be invested in accounts of a bank, savings and loan association, or credit union organized under the laws of this state or federal law, as provided by law.

Section 20. Deposit of State Money in Certain Financial Institutions; Requirements

No state money shall be deposited in banks, savings and loans associations, or credit unions, other than those organized under the law of this state or federal law. No state money shall be deposited in any bank, savings and loan association, or credit union, in excess of 50 percent of the net worth of the bank, savings and loan association, or credit union. Any bank, savings and loan association, or credit union, receiving deposits of state money shall show the amount of state money so deposited as a separate item in all published statements.

Section 21. Accounting for Public Moneys

The legislature shall provide by law for the annual accounting for all public moneys, state and local, and may provide by law for interim accounting. Accounting and auditing for local governments. The legislature shall provide by law for the maintenance of uniform accounting systems by units of local government and the auditing of county accounts by competent state authority and other units of government as provided by law.

Section 22. Examination and Adjustment of Claims Against State

Procedures for the examination and adjustment of claims against the state shall be prescribed by law.

Section 23. Financial Records; Statement of Revenues and Expenditures

All financial records, accountings, audit reports and other reports of public moneys shall be public records and open to inspection. A statement of all revenues and expenditures of public moneys shall be published and distributed annually, as provided by law.

Section 24. Public Pension Plans and Retirement Systems, Obligation

The accrued financial benefits of each pension plan and retirement system of the state and its political subdivisions shall be a contractual obligation thereof which shall not be diminished or impaired thereby.

Financial Benefits, Annual Funding

Financial benefits arising on account of service rendered in each fiscal year shall be funded during that year and such funding shall not be used for financing unfunded accrued liabilities.

Section 25 Voter Approval of Increased Local Taxes; Prohibitions; Emergency Conditions; Repayment of Bonded Indebtedness Guaranteed; Implementation of Section

Property taxes and other local taxes and state taxation and spending may not be increased above the limitations specified herein without direct voter approval. The state is prohibited from requiring any new or expanded activities by local governments without full state financing, from reducing the proportion of state spending in the form of aid to local governments, or from shifting the tax burden to local government. A provision for emergency conditions is established and the repayment of voter approved bonded indebtedness is guaranteed. Implementation of this section is specified in Sections 26 through 34, inclusive, of this Article.

Section 26. Limitation on Taxes; Revenue Limit; Refunding or Transferring Excess Revenues; Exceptions to Revenue Limitation; Adjustment of State Revenue and Spending Limits

There is hereby established a limit on the total amount of taxes which may be imposed by the legislature in any fiscal year on the taxpayers of this state. This limit shall not be changed without approval of the majority of the qualified electors voting thereon, as provided for in Article 12 of the Constitution. Effective with fiscal year 1979-1980, and for each fiscal year thereafter, the legislature shall not impose taxes of any kind which, together with all other revenues of the state, federal aid excluded, exceed the revenue limit established in this section. The revenue limit shall be equal to the product of the ratio of Total State Revenues in fiscal year 1978-79 divided by the Personal Income of Michigan in calendar year 1977 multiplied by the Personal Income of Michigan in either the prior calendar year or the average of Personal Income of Michigan in the previous three calendar years, whichever is greater. For any fiscal year in the event that Total State Revenues exceed the revenue limit established in this section by 1% or more, the excess revenues shall be refunded pro rata based on the liability reported on the Michigan income tax and single business tax (or its successor tax or taxes) annual returns filed following the close of such fiscal year. If the excess is less than 1%, this excess may be transferred to the State Budget Stabilization Fund. The revenue limitation established in this section shall not apply to taxes imposed for the payment of principal and interest on bonds, approved by the voters and authorized under Section 15. of this Article, and loans to school districts authorized under Section 16.

of this Article. If responsibility for funding a program or programs is transferred from one level of government to another, as a consequence of constitutional amendment, the state revenue and spending limits may be adjusted to accommodate such change, provided that the total revenue authorized for collection by both state and local governments does not exceed that amount which would have been authorized without such change.

Section 27. Exceeding Revenue Limit; Conditions

The revenue limit of Section 26 of this Article may be exceeded only if all of the following conditions are met:

(1) The governor requests the legislature to declare an emergency;

(2) the request is specific as to the nature of the emergency, the dollar amount of the emergency, and the method by which the emergency will be funded; and

(3) the legislature thereafter declares an emergency in accordance with the specific of the governor's request by a two-thirds vote of the members elected to and serving in each house. The emergency must be declared in accordance with this section prior to incurring any of the expenses which constitute the emergency request. The revenue limit may be exceeded only during the fiscal year for which the emergency is declared. In no event shall any part of the amount representing a refund under Section 26 of this Article be the subject of an emergency request.

Section 28. Limitation on Expenses of State Government

No expenses of state government shall be incurred in any fiscal year which exceed the sum of the revenue limit established in Sections 26 and 27 of this Article plus federal aid and any surplus from a previous fiscal year.

Section 29. State Financing of Activities or Services Required of Local Government by State Law

The state is hereby prohibited from reducing the state financed proportion of the necessary costs of any existing activity or service required of units of Local Government by state law. A new activity or service or an increase in the level of any activity or service beyond that required by existing law shall not be required by the legislature or any state agency of units of Local Government, unless a state appropriation is made and disbursed to pay the unit of Local Government for any necessary increased costs. The provision of this section shall not apply to costs incurred pursuant to Article VI, Section 18.

Section 30. Reduction of State Spending Paid to Units of Local Government

The proportion of total state spending paid to all units of Local Government, taken as a group, shall not be reduced below that proportion in effect in fiscal year 1978-79.

Section 31. Levying Tax or Increasing Rate of Existing Tax; Maximum Tax Rate on New Base; Increase in Assessed Valuation of Property; Exceptions to Limitations

Units of Local Government are hereby prohibited from levying any tax not authorized by law or charter when this section is ratified or from increasing the rate of an existing tax above that rate authorized by law or charter when this section is ratified, without the approval of a majority of the qualified electors of that unit of Local Government voting thereon. If the definition of the base of an existing tax is broadened, the maximum authorized rate of taxation on the new base in each unit of Local Government shall be reduced to yield the same estimated gross revenue as on the prior base. If the assessed valuation of property as finally equalized, excluding the value of new construction and improvements, increases by a larger percentage than the increase in the General Price Level from the previous year, the maximum authorized rate applied thereto in each unit of Local Government shall be reduced to yield the same gross revenue from existing property, adjusted for changes in the General Price Level, as could have been collected at the existing authorized rate on the prior assessed value. The limitations of this section shall not apply to taxes imposed for the payment of principal and interest on bonds or other evidence of indebtedness or for the payment of assessments on contract obligations in anticipation of which bonds are issued which were authorized prior to the effective date of this amendment.

Section 32. Suit to Enforce Sections 25 To 31

Any taxpayer of the state shall have standing to bring suit in the Michigan State Court of Appeals to enforce the provisions of Sections 25 through 31, inclusive, of this Article and, if the suit is sustained, shall receive from the applicable unit of government his costs incurred in maintaining such suit.

Section 33. Definitions Applicable to Sections 25 To 32

Definitions. The definitions of this section shall apply to Section 25 through 32 of Article IX, inclusive. "Total State Revenues" includes all general and special revenues, excluding federal aid, as defined in the budget message of the governor for fiscal year 1978-1979. Total State Revenues shall exclude the amount of any credits based on actual tax liabilities or the imputed tax components of rental payments, but shall include the amount of any credits not related to actual tax liabilities. "Personal Income of Michigan" is the total income received by persons in Michigan from all sources, as defined and officially reported by the United States Department of Commerce or its successor agency. "Local Government" means any political subdivision of the state, including, but not restricted to, school districts, cities, villages, townships, charter townships, counties, charter counties, authorities created by the state, and authorities created by other units of local government. "General Price Level" means the Consumer Price Index for the United States as defined and officially reported by the United States Department of Labor or its successor agency.

Section 34. Implementation of Sections 25 To 33

The Legislature shall implement the provisions of Sections 25 through 33, inclusive, of this Article.

Section 35. Michigan Natural Resources Trust Fund

There is hereby established the Michigan natural resources trust fund. The trust fund shall consist of all bonuses, rentals, delayed rentals, and royalties collected or reserved by the state under provisions of leases for the extraction of nonrenewable resources from state owned lands, except such revenues accruing under leases of state owned lands acquired with money from state or federal game and fish protection funds or revenues accruing from lands purchased with such revenues. The trust fund may receive appropriations, money, or other things of value. The assets of the trust fund shall be invested as provided by law. Until the trust fund reaches an accumulated principal of $500,000,000.00, $10,000,000.00 of the revenues from bonuses, rentals, delayed rentals, and royalties described in this section otherwise dedicated to the trust fund that are received by the state each state fiscal year shall be deposited into the Michigan state parks endowment fund. However, until the trust fund reaches an accumulated principal of $500,000,000.00, in any state fiscal year, not more than 50 percent of the total revenues from bonuses, rentals, delayed rentals, and royalties described in this section otherwise dedicated to the trust fund that are received by the state each state fiscal year shall be deposited into the Michigan state parks endowment fund. The amount accumulated in the trust fund in any state fiscal year shall not exceed $500,000,000.00, exclusive of interest and earnings and amounts authorized for expenditure pursuant to this section. When the accumulated principal of the trust fund reaches $500,000,000.00, all revenue from bonuses, rentals, delayed rentals, and royalties described in this section that would be received by the trust fund but for this limitation shall be deposited into the Michigan state parks endowment fund until the Michigan state parks endowment fund reaches an accumulated principal of $800,000,000.00. When the Michigan state parks endowment fund reaches an accumulated principal of $800,000,000.00, all revenues from bonuses, rentals, delayed rentals, and royalties described in this section shall be distributed as provided by law. The interest and earnings of the trust fund shall be expended for the acquisition of land or rights in land for recreational uses or protection of the land because of its environmental importance or its scenic beauty, for the development of public recreation facilities, and for the administration of the trust fund, which may include payments in lieu of taxes on state owned land purchased through the trust fund. The trust fund may provide grants to units of local government or public authorities which shall be used for the purposes of this section. The legislature shall provide that a portion of the cost of a project funded by such grants be provided by the local unit of government or public authority. Until the trust fund reaches an accumulated principal of $500,000,000.00, the legislature may provide, in addition to the expenditure of interest and earnings authorized by this section, that a portion, not to exceed 33-1/3 percent, of the revenues from bonuses, rentals, delayed rentals, and royalties described in this section received by the trust fund during each state fiscal year may be expended during subsequent state fiscal years for the purposes of this section. Not less than 25 percent of the total amounts made available for expenditure from the trust fund from any state fiscal year shall be expended for acquisition of land and rights in land and not more than 25 percent of the total amounts made available for expenditure from the trust fund from any state fiscal year shall be expended for development of public recreation facilities. The legislature shall provide by law for the establishment of a trust fund board within the department of natural resources. The trust fund board shall recommend the projects to be funded. The board shall submit its recommendations to the governor who shall submit the board's recommendations to the legislature in an appropriations bill. The legislature shall provide by law for the implementation of this section.

Section 35a. Michigan State Parks Endowment Fund

There is hereby established the Michigan state parks endowment fund. The endowment fund shall consist of revenues as provided in section 35 of this article, and as provided by law. The endowment fund may also receive private contributions of money or other things of value. All money in the Genevieve Gillette state parks endowment fund shall be transferred to the endowment fund. The assets of the endowment fund shall be invested as provided by law. The accumulated principal of the endowment fund shall not exceed $800,000,000.00, which amount shall be annually adjusted pursuant to the rate of inflation beginning when the endowment fund reaches $800,000,000.00. This annually adjusted figure is the accumulated principal limit of the endowment fund. Money available for expenditure from the endowment fund as provided in this section shall be expended for operations, maintenance, and capital improvements at Michigan state parks and for the acquisition of land or rights in land for Michigan state parks. Money in the endowment fund shall be expended as follows:

(1) Until the endowment fund reaches an accumulated principal of $800,000,000.00, each state fiscal year the legislature may appropriate not more than 50 percent of the money received under section 35 of this article plus interest and earnings and any private contributions or other revenue to the endowment fund.

(2) Once the accumulated principal in the endowment fund reaches $800,000,000.00, only the interest and earnings of the endowment fund in excess of the amount necessary to maintain the endowment fund's accumulated principal limit may be made available for expenditure. Unexpended appropriations of the endowment fund from any state fiscal year as authorized by this section may be carried forward or may be appropriated as determined by the legislature for purposes of this section. The legislature shall provide by law for implementation of this section.

Section 36. Tax on Tobacco Products; Dedication of Proceeds

Six percent of the proceeds of the tax on tobacco products shall be dedicated to improving the quality of health care of the residents of this state.

Section 37. Michigan Veterans Trust Fund

The Michigan veterans' trust fund is established within the department of treasury. All money in the fund established by 1946 (1st Ex Sess) PA 9 shall be transferred to the Michigan veterans' trust fund. The trust fund may additionally receive appropriations, money, or other things of value. The state treasurer shall direct investment of the fund as provided by law, and credit interest and earnings of the fund to the fund. Except for the state treasurer's actions authorized under this section, an expenditure or transfer of a trust fund asset, interest, or earnings may be made only upon the authorization of a majority of the members of the Michigan veterans' trust fund board of trustees.

Section 38. Michigan Veterans Trust Fund Board Of Trustees; Establishment

The Michigan veterans' trust fund board of trustees is established and consists of veterans honorably discharged from the armed services and appointed by the governor as prescribed by law.

Section 39. Michigan Veterans Trust Fund Board of Trustees; Administration Of Trust Fund

The Michigan veterans' trust fund board of trustees shall administer the Michigan veterans' trust fund. The board of trustees shall not authorize the expenditure or transfer of a trust fund asset, interest, or earnings unless the board of trustees determines in its discretion and by a majority vote that the expenditure or transfer is for the benefit of veterans or their spouses or dependents.

Section 40. Michigan Conservation and Recreation Legacy Fund

The Michigan conservation and recreation legacy fund is established. The state treasurer shall direct the investment of the legacy fund. The state treasurer shall establish within the legacy fund restricted accounts as authorized by this section and may establish additional subaccounts as authorized by law. The state treasurer may receive gifts, grants, bequests, or assets from any source for deposit into a particular account or subaccount. The assets of the legacy fund shall be invested as provided by law. Interest and earnings accruing from each account or subaccount shall be credited to that account or subaccount. The forest recreation account is established as an account within the legacy fund. The forest recreation account shall consist of revenue derived from concessions, leases, contracts, and fees from recreational activities on state forestlands and other revenues as authorized by law. Money in the forest recreation account shall be expended only for the following:

(a) The development, improvement, operation, promotion, and maintenance of forest recreation activities.

(b) Grants to state colleges and universities to implement programs funded by the forest recreation account.

(c) The administration of the forest recreation account. The game and fish protection account is established as an account within the legacy fund. The game and fish protection account shall consist of revenue derived from hunting and fishing licenses, passbooks, permits, fees, concessions, leases, contracts, and activities; damages paid for the illegal taking of game and fish; revenue derived from fees, licenses, and permits related to game, game areas, and game fish; and other revenues as authorized by law. Money in the game and fish protection account shall be expended only for the following:

(a) The development, improvement, operation, promotion, and maintenance of wildlife and fisheries programs and facilities.

(b) The acquisition of land and rights in land that support wildlife and fisheries programs.

(c) Research to support wildlife and fisheries programs.

(d) The enforcement and administration of the wildlife and fisheries laws of the state, including the necessary equipment and apparatus incident to the operation and enforcement of wildlife and fisheries laws.

(e) The protection, propagation, distribution, and control of wildlife and fish.

(f) Grants to state colleges and universities to implement programs funded by the game and fish protection account.

(g) The administration of the game and fish protection account, which may include payments in lieu of taxes on state owned land that has been or will be purchased through the game and fish protection fund or account. The off-road vehicle account is established as an account within the legacy fund. The off-road vehicle account shall consist of revenue derived from fees imposed upon the use or registration of off-road vehicles and other revenues as authorized by law. Money in the off-road vehicle account shall be expended only for the following:

(a) Signage for and the improvement, maintenance, and construction of off-road vehicle trails, routes, or areas.

(b) The administration and enforcement of state regulations related to off-road vehicles.

(c) The leasing of land for use by off-road vehicles.

(d) The acquisition of easements, permits, or other agreements for the use of land for off-road vehicle trails, routes, or areas.

(e) The restoration of any of the natural resources of the state on public land that are damaged due to off-road vehicle use.

(f) Safety education programs related to the operation of off-road vehicles.

(g) Other uses as provided by law as long as the uses are consistent with the development, improvement, operation, promotion, and maintenance of the state's off-road vehicle programs.

(h) Grants to state colleges and universities to implement programs funded by the off-road vehicle account.

(i) The administration of the off-road vehicle account. The recreation improvement account is established as an account within the legacy fund. The recreation improvement account shall consist of all tax revenue derived from the sale of two percent of the gasoline sold in this state for consumption in internal combustion engines and other revenues as authorized by law. Money in the recreation improvement account shall be distributed as follows:

(a) Eighty percent of the money shall be annually transferred to the waterways account to be used for the purposes of that account.

(b) Fourteen percent of the money shall be annually transferred to the snowmobile account to be used for the purposes of that account.

(c) The remainder of the money that is not transferred under this section shall be used, upon appropriation, for recreation projects, including grants to state colleges and universities to implement recreation projects, and for the administration of the recreation improvement account. Of the amount that is credited to recreational projects in a fiscal year, not less than twenty-five percent of any funds designated for projects intended for off-road vehicles shall be expended on projects to repair damages as a result of pollution, impairment, or destruction of air, water, or other natural resources, or the public trust, in air, water, or other natural resources, as a result of the use of off-road vehicles. The snowmobile account is established as an account within the legacy fund. The snowmobile account shall consist of revenue derived from fees imposed for the registration or use of snowmobiles; revenue derived from the use of snowmobile trails; transfers from the recreation improvement account; and other revenues as authorized by law. Money in the snowmobile account shall be expended only for the following:

(a) Planning, construction, maintenance, and acquisition of trails and areas for the use of snowmobiles.

(b) Providing access to trails and areas for the use of snowmobiles.

(c) Providing basic snowmobile facilities.

(d) The administration and enforcement of state regulations related to snowmobiles.

(e) Safety education programs related to the operation of snowmobiles.

(f) Other uses as provided by law as long as the uses are consistent with the development, improvement, operation, promotion, and maintenance of the state's snowmobile programs.

(g) Grants to state colleges and universities to implement programs funded by the snowmobile account.

(h) The administration of the snowmobile account, which may include payments in lieu of taxes on state owned land that has been or will be purchased through the recreational snowmobile trail improvement fund or snowmobile account. The state park improvement account is established as an account within the legacy fund. The state park improvement account shall consist of revenue derived from concessions, leases, contracts, fees, and permits for activities in state parks and recreation areas; damages paid to the state for illegal activities in state parks and recreation areas; and other revenues as authorized by law. Money in the state park improvement account shall be expended only for the following:

(a) The development, improvement, operation, promotion, and maintenance of state parks and recreation areas.

(b) Grants to state colleges and universities to implement programs funded by the state park improvement account.

(c) The administration of the state park improvement account. The waterways account is established as an account within the legacy fund. The waterways account shall consist of revenue derived from watercraft registration fees assessed on the ownership or operation of watercraft in the state; revenue derived from fees charged for the moorage of watercraft at state-operated mooring facilities; revenue derived from fees charged for the use of state-operated public access sites; transfers from the recreation improvement account; all tax revenue derived from the sale of diesel fuel in this state that is used to generate power for the operation or propulsion of vessels on the waterways of the state; and other revenues as authorized by law. Money in the waterways account shall be expended only for the following:

(a) The construction, operation, and maintenance of recreational boating facilities that provide public access to waterways or moorage of watercraft.

(b) The acquisition of property for the purpose of paragraph (a).

(c) Grants to local units of government and state colleges and universities for the provision of public access or moorage of watercraft and law enforcement or boating education to recreational watercraft operators.

(d) The acquisition and development of harbors and public access sites.

(e) The enforcement of laws related to the operation of watercraft and education related to the operation of watercraft. Not less than forty-nine percent of revenues from watercraft registration fees received by the waterways account shall be used for the purposes of this subdivision.

(f) The administration of programs funded by the waterways account.

(g) Other uses as provided by law as long as the uses are consistent with the development, improvement, operation, promotion, and maintenance of the state's waterways programs.

(h) The administration of the waterways account, which may include payments in lieu of taxes on state owned land that has been or will be purchased through the Michigan state waterways fund or waterways account. The legislature shall provide by law for the implementation of this section.

Section 41. Michigan Game and Fish Protection Trust Fund

The Michigan game and fish protection trust fund is established. The Michigan game and fish protection trust fund shall consist of revenue derived from bonuses, rentals, delayed rentals, royalties, and other revenues collected or reserved by the state under leases or direct sale contracts accruing from state owned lands acquired with money from state or federal game and fish protection funds or revenues accruing from lands purchased with such revenues. The Michigan game and fish protection trust fund may also receive gifts, grants, bequests, or assets from any source and may receive other revenues as authorized by law. The assets of the Michigan game and fish protection trust fund shall be invested as provided by law. The interest and earnings from these investments shall be credited to the Michigan game and fish protection trust fund. The accumulated interest and earnings of the Michigan game and fish protection trust fund and not more than $6,000,000.00 of the principal of the Michigan game and fish protection trust fund may be expended in any year for the purposes of the game and fish protection account of the Michigan conservation and recreation legacy fund established in section 40. The legislature shall provide by law for the implementation of this section.

Section 42. Michigan Nongame Fish and Wildlife Trust Fund

The Michigan nongame fish and wildlife trust fund is established. The Michigan nongame fish and wildlife trust fund shall consist of revenue designated by a member of the public for the benefit of nongame fish and wildlife. The Michigan nongame fish and wildlife trust fund may also receive gifts, grants, bequests, or assets from any source and may receive other revenues as authorized by law. The assets of the Michigan nongame fish and wildlife trust fund shall be invested as provided by law. The interest and earnings from these investments shall be credited to the Michigan nongame fish and wildlife trust fund. The Michigan nongame fish and wildlife trust fund shall maintain a principal balance of not less than $6,000,000.00. The interest and earnings of the Michigan nongame fish and wildlife trust fund and other revenues not retained on a permanent basis shall be expended only for the following:

(a) The management of nongame fish and wildlife species consistent with a long-range plan for the management of Michigan's nongame fish and wildlife resources.

(b) Grants to state colleges and universities to implement programs funded by the Michigan nongame fish and wildlife trust fund.

(c) The administration of the Michigan nongame fish and wildlife trust fund.

ARTICLE X: PROPERTY

Section 1. Disabilities of Coverture Abolished; Separate Property Of Wife; Dower

The disabilities of coverture as to property are abolished. The real and personal estate of every woman acquired before marriage and all real and personal property to which she may afterwards become entitled shall be and remain the estate and property of such woman, and shall not be liable for the debts, obligations or engagements of her husband, and may be dealt with and disposed of by her as if she were unmarried. Dower may be relinquished or conveyed as provided by law.

Section 2. Eminent Domain; Compensation

Private property shall not be taken for public use without just compensation therefore being first made or secured in a manner prescribed by law. If private property consisting of an individual's principal residence is taken for public use, the amount of compensation made and determined for that taking shall be not less than 125% of that property's fair market value, in addition to any other reimbursement allowed by law. Compensation shall be determined in proceedings in a court of record. "Public use" does not include the taking of private property for transfer to a private entity for the purpose of economic development or enhancement of tax revenues. Private property otherwise may be taken for reasons of public use as that term is understood on the effective date of the amendment to this constitution that added this paragraph. In a condemnation action, the burden of proof is on the condemning authority to demonstrate, by the preponderance of the evidence, that the taking of a private property is for a public use, unless the condemnation action involves a taking for the eradication of blight, in which case the burden of proof is on the condemning authority to demonstrate, by clear and convincing evidence, that the taking of that property is for a public use. (146) Any existing right, grant, or benefit afforded to property owners as of November 1, 2005, whether provided by this section, by statute, or otherwise, shall be preserved and shall not be abrogated or impaired by the constitutional amendment that added this paragraph.

Section 3. Homestead and Personalty, Exemption from Process

A homestead in the amount of not less than $3,500 and personal property of every resident of this state in the amount of not less than $750, as defined by law, shall be exempt from forced sale on execution or other process of any court. Such exemptions shall not extend to any lien thereon excluded from exemption by law.

Section 4. Escheats

Procedures relating to escheats and to the custody and disposition of escheated property shall be prescribed by law.

Section 5. State Lands

The legislature shall have general supervisory jurisdiction over all state owned lands useful for forest preserves, game areas and recreational purposes; shall require annual reports as to such lands from all departments having supervision or control thereof; and shall by general law provide for the sale, lease or other disposition of such lands.

State Land Reserve

The legislature by an act adopted by two-thirds of the members elected to and serving in each house may designate any part of such lands as a state land reserve. No lands in the state land reserve may be removed from the reserve, sold, leased or otherwise disposed of except by an act of the legislature.

Section 6. Resident Aliens, Property Rights

Aliens who are residents of this state shall enjoy the same rights and privileges in property as citizens of this state.

ARTICLE XI: PUBLIC OFFICERS AND EMPLOYMENT

Section 1. Oath of Public Officers

All officers, legislative, executive and judicial, before entering upon the duties of their respective offices, shall take and subscribe the following oath or affirmation: I do solemnly swear (or affirm) that I will support the Constitution of the United States and the constitution of this state, and that I will faithfully discharge the duties of the office of .... according to the best of my ability. No other oath, affirmation, or any religious test shall be required as a qualification for any office or public trust.

Section 2. Terms of Office of State and County Officers

The terms of office of elective state officers, members of the legislature and justices and judges of courts of record shall begin at twelve o'clock noon on the first day of January next succeeding their election, except as otherwise provided in this constitution. The terms of office of county officers shall begin on the first day of January next succeeding their election, except as otherwise provided by law.

Section 3. Extra Compensation

Neither the legislature nor any political subdivision of this state shall grant or authorize extra compensation to any public officer, agent or contractor after the service has been rendered or the contract entered into.

Section 4. Custodian of Public Moneys; Eligibility To Office, Accounting

No person having custody or control of public moneys shall be a member of the legislature, or be eligible to any office of trust or profit under this state, until he shall have made an accounting, as provided by law, of all sums for which he may be liable.

Section 5. Classified State Civil Service; Scope; Exempted Positions; Appointment And Terms Of Members Of State Civil Service Commission; State Personnel Director; Duties Of Commission; Collective Bargaining For State Police Troopers And Sergeants; Appointments, Promotions, Demotions, Or Removals; Increases Or Reductions In Compensation; Creating Or Abolishing Positions; Recommending Compensation For Unclassified Service; Appropriation; Reports Of Expenditures; Annual Audit; Payment For Personal Services; Violation; Injunctive Or Mandamus Proceedings

The classified state civil service shall consist of all positions in the state service except those filled by popular election, heads of principal departments, members of boards and commissions, the principal executive officer of boards and commissions heading principal departments, employees of courts of record, employees of the legislature, employees of the state institutions of higher education, all persons in the armed forces of the state, eight exempt positions in the office of the governor, and within each principal department, when requested by the department head, two other exempt positions, one of which shall be policy-making. The civil service commission may exempt three additional positions of a policy-making nature within each principal department. The civil service commission shall be non-salaried and shall consist of four persons, not more than two of whom shall be members of the same political party, appointed by the governor for terms of eight years, no two of which shall expire in the same year. The administration of the commission's powers shall be vested in a state personnel director who shall be a member of the classified service and who shall be responsible to and selected by the commission after open competitive examination. The commission shall classify all positions in the classified service according to their respective duties and responsibilities, fix rates of compensation for all classes of positions, approve or disapprove disbursements for all personal services, determine by competitive examination and performance exclusively on the basis of merit, efficiency and fitness the qualifications of all candidates for positions in the classified service, make rules and regulations covering all personnel transactions, and regulate all conditions of employment in the classified service. State Police Troopers and Sergeants shall, through their elected representative designated by 50% of such troopers and sergeants, have the right to bargain collectively with their employer concerning conditions of their employment, compensation, hours, working conditions, retirement, pensions, and other aspects of employment except promotions which will be determined by competitive examination and performance on the basis of merit, efficiency and fitness; and they shall have the right 30 days after commencement of such bargaining to submit any unresolved disputes to binding arbitration for the resolution thereof the same as now provided by law for Public Police and Fire Departments. No person shall be appointed to or promoted in the classified service who has not been certified by the commission as qualified for such appointment or promotion. No appointments, promotions, demotions or removals in the classified service shall be made for religious, racial or partisan considerations. Increases in rates of compensation authorized by the commission may be effective only at the start of a fiscal year and shall require prior notice to the governor, who shall transmit such increases to the legislature as part of his budget. The legislature may, by a majority vote of the members elected to and serving in each house, waive the notice and permit increases in rates of compensation to be effective at a time other than the start of a fiscal year. Within 60 calendar days following such transmission, the legislature may, by a two-thirds vote of the members elected to and serving in each house, reject or reduce increases in rates of compensation authorized by the commission. Any reduction ordered by the legislature shall apply uniformly to all classes of employees affected by the increases and shall not adjust pay differentials already established by the civil service commission. The legislature may not reduce rates of compensation below those in effect at the time of the transmission of increases authorized by the commission. The appointing authorities may create or abolish positions for reasons of administrative efficiency without the approval of the commission. Positions shall not be created nor abolished except for reasons of administrative efficiency. Any employee considering himself aggrieved by the abolition or creation of a position shall have a right of appeal to the commission through established grievance procedures. The civil service commission shall recommend to the governor and to the legislature rates of compensation for all appointed positions within the executive department not a part of the classified service. To enable the commission to exercise its powers, the legislature shall appropriate to the commission for the ensuing fiscal year a sum not less than one percent of the aggregate payroll of the classified service for the preceding fiscal year, as certified by the commission. Within six months after the conclusion of each fiscal year the commission shall return to the state treasury all moneys unexpended for that fiscal year. The commission shall furnish reports of expenditures, at least annually, to the governor and the legislature and shall be subject to annual audit as provided by law. No payment for personal services shall be made or authorized until the provisions of this constitution pertaining to civil service have been complied with in every particular. Violation of any of the provisions hereof may be restrained or observance compelled by injunctive or mandamus proceedings brought by any citizen of the state.

Section 6. Merit Systems for Local Governments

By ordinance or resolution of its governing body which shall not take effect until approved by a majority of the electors voting thereon, unless otherwise provided by charter, each county, township, city, village, school district and other governmental unit or authority may establish, modify or discontinue a merit system for its employees other than teachers under contract or tenure. The state civil service commission may on request furnish technical services to any such unit on a reimbursable basis.

Section 7. Impeachment of Civil Officers

The house of representatives shall have the sole power of impeaching civil officers for corrupt conduct in office or for crimes or misdemeanors, but a majority of the members elected thereto and serving therein shall be necessary to direct an impeachment.

Prosecution by 3 Members of House of Representatives

When an impeachment is directed, the house of representatives shall elect three of its members to prosecute the impeachment.

Trial by Senate; Oath, Presiding Officer

Every impeachment shall be tried by the senate immediately after the final adjournment of the legislature. The senators shall take an oath or affirmation truly and impartially to try and determine the impeachment according to the evidence. When the governor or lieutenant governor is tried, the chief justice of the supreme court shall preside.

Conviction; Vote, Penalty

No person shall be convicted without the concurrence of two-thirds of the senators elected and serving. Judgment in case of conviction shall not extend further than removal from office, but the person convicted shall be liable to punishment according to law.

Judicial Officers, Functions After Impeachment

No judicial officer shall exercise any of the functions of his office after an impeachment is directed until he is acquitted.

Section 8. Convictions for Certain Felonies; Eligibility for Elective Office or Certain Positions of Public Employment

A person is ineligible for election or appointment to any state or local elective office of this state and ineligible to hold a position in public employment in this state that is policy-making or that has discretionary authority over public assets if, within the immediately preceding 20 years, the person was convicted of a felony involving dishonesty, deceit, fraud, or a breach of the public trust and the conviction was related to the person's official capacity while the person was holding any elective office or position of employment in local, state, or federal government. This requirement is in addition to any other qualification required under this constitution or by law. The legislature shall prescribe by law for the implementation of this section.

ARTICLE XII: AMENDMENT AND REVISION

Section 1. Amendment by Legislative Proposal and Vote of Electors

Amendments to this constitution may be proposed in the senate or house of representatives. Proposed amendments agreed to by two-thirds of the members elected to and serving in each house on a vote with the names and vote of those voting entered in the respective journals shall be submitted, not less than 60 days thereafter, to the electors at the next general election or special election as the legislature shall direct. If a majority of electors voting on a proposed amendment approve the same, it shall become part of the constitution and shall abrogate or amend existing provisions of the constitution at the end of 45 days after the date of the election at which it was approved.

Section 2. Amendment by Petition and Vote of Electors

Amendments may be proposed to this constitution by petition of the registered electors of this state. Every petition shall include the full text of the proposed amendment, and be signed by registered electors of the state equal in number to at least 10 percent of the total vote cast for all candidates for governor at the last preceding general election at which a governor was elected. Such petitions shall be filed with the person authorized by law to receive the same at least 120 days before the election at which the proposed amendment is to be voted upon. Any such petition shall be in the form, and shall be signed and circulated in such manner, as prescribed by law. The person authorized by law to receive such petition shall upon its receipt determine, as provided by law, the validity and sufficiency of the signatures on the petition, and make an official announcement thereof at least 60 days prior to the election at which the proposed amendment is to be voted upon.

Submission of Proposal; Publication

Any amendment proposed by such petition shall be submitted, not less than 120 days after it was filed, to the electors at the next general election. Such proposed amendment, existing provisions of the constitution which would be altered or abrogated thereby, and the question as it shall appear on the ballot shall be published in full as provided by law. Copies of such publication shall be posted in each polling place and furnished to news media as provided by law.

Ballot, Statement of Purpose

The ballot to be used in such election shall contain a statement of the purpose of the proposed amendment, expressed in not more than 100 words, exclusive of caption. Such statement of purpose and caption shall be prepared by the person authorized by law, and shall consist of a true and impartial statement of the purpose of the amendment in such language as shall create no prejudice for or against the proposed amendment.

Approval of Proposal, Effective Date; Conflicting Amendments

If the proposed amendment is approved by a majority of the electors voting on the question, it shall become part of the constitution, and shall abrogate or amend existing provisions of the constitution at the end of 45 days after the date of the election at which it was approved. If two or more amendments approved by the electors at the same election conflict, that amendment receiving the highest affirmative vote shall prevail.

Section 3. General Revision of Constitution; Submission of Question, Convention Delegates and Meeting

At the general election to be held in the year 1978, and in each 16th year thereafter and at such times as may be provided by law, the question of a general revision of the constitution shall be submitted to the electors of the state. If a majority of the electors voting on the question decide in favor of a convention for such purpose, at an election to be held not later than six months after the proposal was certified as approved, the electors of each representative district as then organized shall elect one delegate and the electors of each senatorial district as then organized shall elect one delegate at a partisan election. The delegates so elected shall convene at the seat of government on the first Tuesday in October next succeeding such election or at an earlier date if provided by law.

Convention Officers, Rules, Membership, Personnel, Publications

The convention shall choose its own officers, determine the rules of its proceedings and judge the qualifications, elections and returns of its members. To fill a vacancy in the office of any delegate, the governor shall appoint a qualified resident of the same district who shall be a member of the same party as the delegate vacating the office. The convention shall have power to appoint such officers, employees and assistants as it deems necessary and to fix their compensation; to provide for the printing and distribution of its documents, journals and proceedings; to explain and disseminate information about the proposed constitution and to complete the business of the convention in an orderly manner. Each delegate shall receive for his services compensation provided by law.

Submission of Proposed Constitution or Amendment

No proposed constitution or amendment adopted by such convention shall be submitted to the electors for approval as hereinafter provided unless by the assent of a majority of all the delegates elected to and serving in the convention, with the names and vote of those voting entered in the journal. Any proposed constitution or amendments adopted by such convention shall be submitted to the qualified electors in the manner and at the time provided by such convention not less than 90 days after final adjournment of the convention. Upon the approval of such constitution or amendments by a majority of the qualified electors voting thereon the constitution or amendments shall take effect as provided by the convention.

Section 4. Severability

If any section, subsection or part of Article 2, Section 10, Article 4, Section 54 or Article 5, Section 30 is for any reason held to be invalid or unconstitutional, the remaining sections, subsections or parts of those sections shall not be affected but will remain in full force and effect.

SCHEDULE AND TEMPORARY PROVISIONS

To insure the orderly transition from the constitution of 1908 to this constitution the following schedule and temporary provisions are set forth to be effective for such period as are thereby required.

Section 1. Recommendations by Attorney General for Changes in Laws

The attorney general shall recommend to the legislature as soon as practicable such changes as may be necessary to adapt existing laws to this constitution.

Section 2. Existing Public and Private Rights, Continuance

All writs, actions, suits, proceedings, civil or criminal liabilities, prosecutions, judgments, sentences, orders, decrees, appeals, causes of action, contracts, claims, demands, titles and rights existing on the effective date of this constitution shall continue unaffected except as modified in accordance with the provisions of this constitution.

Section 3. Officers, Continuance in Office

Except as otherwise provided in this constitution, all officers filling any office by election or appointment shall continue to exercise their powers and duties until their offices shall have been abolished or their successors selected and qualified in accordance with this constitution or the laws enacted pursuant thereto.

Terms of Office

No provision of this constitution, or of law or of executive order authorized by this constitution shall shorten the term of any person elected to state office at a statewide election on or prior to the date on which this constitution is submitted to a vote. In the event the duties of any such officers shall not have been abolished or incorporated into one or more of the principal departments at the expiration of his term, such officer shall continue to serve until his duties are so incorporated or abolished.

Section 4. Officers Elected in Spring of 1963, Term

All officers elected at the same election that this constitution is submitted to the people for adoption shall take office and complete the term to which they were elected under the 1908 constitution and existing laws and continue to serve until their successors are elected and qualified pursuant to this constitution or law.

Section 5. State Elective Executive Officers and Senators, 2 and 4 Year Terms

Notwithstanding any other provision in this constitution, the governor, the lieutenant governor, the secretary of state, the attorney general and state senators shall be elected at the general election in 1964 to serve for two-year terms beginning on the first day of January next succeeding their election. The first election of such officers for four-year terms under this constitution shall be held at the general election in 1966.

Section 6. Supreme Court, Reduction to 7 Justices

Notwithstanding the provisions of this constitution that the supreme court shall consist of seven justices it shall consist of eight justices until the time that a vacancy occurs as a result of death, retirement or resignation of a justice. The first such vacancy shall not be filled.

Section 7. Judges of Probate, Eligibility for Re-Election

Any judge of probate serving on the effective date of this constitution may serve the remainder of the term and be eligible to succeed himself for election regardless of other provisions in this constitution requiring him to be licensed to practice law in this state.

Section 8. Judicial Officers, Staggered Terms

The provisions of Article VI providing that terms of judicial offices shall not all expire at the same time, shall be implemented by law providing that at the next election for such offices judges shall be elected for terms of varying length, none of which shall be shorter than the regular term provided for the office.

Section 9. State Board of Education; First Election, Terms

The members of the state board of education provided for in Section 3. of Article VIII of this constitution shall first be elected at the first general election after the effective date of this constitution for the following terms: two shall be elected for two years, two for four years, two for six years, and two for eight years as prescribed by law.

Abolition of Existing State Board of Education

The state board of education provided for in the constitution of 1908 is abolished at twelve o'clock noon January 1 of the year following the first general election under this constitution and the terms of members thereof shall then expire.

Section 10. Boards Controlling Higher Education Institutions and State Board of Public Community and Junior Colleges, Terms

The provisions of this constitution providing for members of boards of control of institutions of higher education and the state board of public community and junior colleges shall be implemented by law. The law may provide that the term of each member in office on the date of the vote on this constitution may be extended, and may further provide that the initial terms of office of members may be less than eight years.

Section 11. Michigan State University Trustees and Wayne State University Governors, Terms

The provisions of this constitution increasing the number of members of the Board of Trustees of Michigan State University and the Board of Governors of Wayne State University to eight, and of their term of office to eight years, shall be implemented by law. The law may provide that the term of each member in office on the date of the vote on this constitution may be extended one year, and may further provide that the initial terms of office of the additional members may be less than eight years.

Section 12. Initial Allocation of Departments by Law or Executive Order

The initial allocation of departments by law pursuant to Section 2. of Article V of this constitution, shall be completed within two years after the effective date of this constitution. If such allocation shall not have been completed within such period, the governor, within one year thereafter, by executive order, shall make the initial allocation.

Section 13. State Contracts, Continuance

Contractual obligations of the state incurred pursuant to the constitution of 1908 shall continue to be obligations of the state.

Section 14. Mackinac Bridge Authority; Refunding of Bonds, Transfer of Functions to Highway Department

The legislature by a vote of two-thirds of the members elected to and serving in each house may provide that the state may borrow money and may pledge its full faith and credit for refunding any bonds issued by the Mackinac Bridge Authority and at the time of refunding the Mackinac Bridge Authority shall be abolished and the operation of the bridge shall be assumed by the state highway department. The legislature may implement this section by law.

Section 15. Submission of Constitution; Time, Notice

This constitution shall be submitted to the people for their adoption or rejection at the general election to be held on the first Monday in April, 1963. It shall be the duty of the secretary of state forthwith to give notice of such submission to all other officers required to give or publish any notice in regard to a general election. He shall give notice that this constitution will be duly submitted to the electors at such election. The notice shall be given in the manner required for the election of governor.

Section 16. Voters, Ballots, Effective Date

Every registered elector may vote on the adoption of the constitution. The board of election commissioners in each county shall cause to be printed on a ballot separate from the ballot containing the names of the nominees for office, the words: Shall the revised constitution be adopted? ( ) Yes. ( ) No. All votes cast at the election shall be taken, counted, canvassed and returned as provided by law for the election of state officers. If the revised constitution so submitted receives more votes in its favor than were cast against it, it shall be the supreme law of the state on and after the first day of January of the year following its adoption.

Adopted by the Constitutional Convention of nineteen hundred sixty-one at Constitution Hall in Lansing on the first day of August, nineteen hundred sixty-two.

www.ingramcontent.com/pod-product-compliance
Lightning Source LLC
Chambersburg PA
CBHW052302220526
45471CB00001B/449